His Cold Feet

His Cold Feet

A Guide for

the Woman Who

Wants to Tie the

Knot with the Guy

Who Wants to Talk

About It Later

Andrea Passman Candell

with Cheryl Fenton

 St. Martin's Griffin ☗ New York

HIS COLD FEET. Copyright © 2008 by Andrea Passman Candell. All
rights reserved. Printed in the United States of America. No part of this
book may be used or reproduced in any manner whatsoever without
written permission except in the case of brief quotations embodied in
critical articles or reviews. For information, address St. Martin's Press,
175 Fifth Avenue, New York, N.Y. 10010.

www.stmartins.com

Book design by Michelle McMillian

Library of Congress Cataloging-in-Publication Data
Candell, Andrea Passman.
His cold feet : a guide for the woman who wants to tie the knot with
the guy who wants to talk about it later / Andrea Passman Candell with
Cheryl Fenton.—1st ed.
     p. cm
Includes bibliographical references.
ISBN-13: 978-0-312-36213-3
ISBN-10: 0-312-36213-7
     1. Man-woman relationships. 2. Interpersonal communication.
3. Sex differences (Psychology) 4. Men—Psychology. 5. Women
Psychology. I. Fenton, Cheryl. II. Title.

HQ801.C2753   2008
306.73'4—dc22   2007039754

First Edition: February 2008

10 9 8 7 6 5 4 3 2 1

To my husband, Scot,
whose feet inspired this book

Contents

Acknowledgments

THANK YOU TO:

Literary agent Jennifer DeChiara—you sure do make dreams come true. Thank you for everything that you do and for taking me under your wing!

Editor Jennifer Enderlin, for this opportunity. I feel so fortunate to be working with you on this book—*thank you!*

My husband, Scot. You are my home sweet home. Thank you for all of your support and insight—I couldn't have written this book without you!

Jake, for lighting up our lives—you are my greatest teacher.

Cheryl Fenton, for working with me on this and for adding your wit and magic to these pages. You're an inspiration!

Dr. Judye Hess, for teaching couples therapy at the California Institute of Integral Studies with such passion and for all of the wisdom you contributed to this book.

Dr. Beth Miller, for all of your fabulous tips and for being such a special part of *His Cold Feet*.

Caitlin Manning, for giving me a tour of Dogpatch, U.S.A.

Mom, for listening whenever I had just one more thing to run by you, no matter what time of night. Dad, for cheering me on as much as you've rooted for the Red Sox—and for telling everyone you meet about HisColdFeet.com. My brother, Scott, for teaching me that "good things come from hard work." Nana Pearl and Papa Mort, for telling me to put the big rocks in first and to "b.a.g.k." Aunt Bev Levy, for proofreading many pages and for always getting back to me in a New York minute, and to Uncle John, for all of the great advice along the way. Allison Baker Cohen, for helping me through my own limbo and for always being more like a sister to me—you're a true soul-friend! Hillary Koritz Price, for making the remarkable even more so. Hyun Ju and Sean Minton, for always going above and beyond!! My in-laws—Sue, for always wanting to read my drafts, and Steve, for all the encouragement. Matt Ranen, Jennifer Coffey, and the Silent Writing Group. Jessica Mullens, Deborah Gleken, and my cousin Tiffany Woolf for helping to kick off the HisColdFeet.com Web site. Tiffany, thanks for always being there just at the right time, "We're family!" And thanks to "the committee of girlfriends," friends, and family.

A very special thank-you to Dave and all of the women for supporting each other on the HisColdFeet.com message board. And to Kevin Burke of Defending the Caveman for his Q & A page on HisColdFeet.com.

Thanks also go to AskMen.com, BestWeddingSites.com, Ultimate Weddings.com, WeddingSolutions.com, Yelp.com, and others for letting me spread the word to your visitors that I wanted to hear their pre-engagement stories. And to everyone who either filled out a questionnaire or put me in touch with a friend to interview—thank you! Most of all, thank you to everyone who shared your pre-engagement story with me (I won't print your name)!

Miss you, Aunt Jo-Ann Srivastava and Auntie Anne Woolf.

—Andrea

A THANK-YOU FROM CHERYL FENTON:

To my husband, Keith. I'm sure it wasn't easy for you to see this manuscript hanging around the house when you and I were going through our own pre-engagement limbo. Thanks for always having a sense of humor with it. Let's always be newlyweds. I love you. Ever Never.

To Andrea, for taking a friendship, an idea, and a talent, and mixing them into one amazing adventure. I've loved every minute of the journey and look forward to more.

To Whitney. Always my rock. Always my friend.

To Mom and Dad, for . . . well . . . everything. What can I say that hasn't been said before? I love you.

To Cadence, the reason for all my smiles.

—Cheryl

His Cold Feet

Why I Engaged in Writing This Book

I thought it would be like a
romance novel. He would sweep
me off my feet, love in the air, a
ring on my finger. But it wasn't
that easy. It turned into a Dick
and Jane book. A bit more like
See Dick Run. He wasn't ready
when I was. So I waited. He would
avoid things. We got engaged
eventually, but it was a long,
frustrating road.

—SARA, 34

My husband and I were sharing a milk shake at our favorite veggie burger place in San Francisco when it happened. Right at the table next to us, a woman (let's call her Jane) and her boyfriend were talking about getting married. She brought up getting engaged; he started lacing up his running shoes.

Then I heard Jane pop her own question: "So when do you think we're going to get engaged?" Time stood still. These words were so powerful, and yet so intimate. Hearing them caught my undivided and unwanted attention. I was sucked into their life's saga.

I could tell this wasn't a first for this discussion topic. No, no . . . this was a tango that these two had danced before. But they were clearly still out of sync. Those of us who have been on that empty stage ourselves recognize the awkward dance. The body language, facial expressions, and nervous voices. They're dead giveaways that create an intriguing mix of bored been-there-done-that and hopeful maybe-this-time-will-be-different.

Jane sat with a straight back, elbows on the table in a professional stiffness, ready to charge, yet exhausted from twirling and twirling around this topic. Her partner was leaning as far back from the table as his body would allow him without falling out of his seat. This was the last place he wanted to be. It was obvious that they knew the steps, but the tempos were off. She was racing forward. He liked the slower beat.

While reaching for the fries, Jane continued with the familiar litany: "All of our friends are getting engaged. We've been together the longest, and each time after we talk about this, I still don't get what you're thinking."

With hesitation and careful thought, her partner muttered, "Do we have to talk about this again? Why do you always have to bring this up?"

I was compelled to stay tuned to this drama–comedy–horror show. It was better than *Sex and the City*. Actually, this could have been on *Sex and the City*! I watched their perplexed faces and tried to read their minds. Her thoughts: "Why am I still in this relationship?" His thoughts: "Why does she bring this up every day?"

He looked pathetically back at her and finally said, "I want to get married, and I want to marry you. I just don't feel ready yet. I want to feel ready."

She wanted to know when he was going to be ready. How would he know? Would he get a special twinkle in his eyes? Would his turkey popper pop? Would the sky open with angels singing and a beam of sunlight cascading at his feet? Even I, an innocent bystander, wanted to know what "ready" feels like.

I never got to hear the end of their saga. Before I knew it, our check had arrived and we had twenty minutes to spare before our movie time. Not hearing the story's finale felt like someone had ripped the best mystery novel ever out of my hands, right before I found out the who-done-it (or even the did-he-ever-do-it!).

DANCING THE LIMBO

I've logged in many hours consoling frustrated women (myself included) who have been in Jane's shoes, a pair of skyscraper five-inch heels that leave us teetering on the edge of confusion and frustration.

A woman who wants to get engaged to a boyfriend who isn't ready creates the perfect recipe for conflict and intense emotions. And where did I start to notice this conflict the most? Short of being advertised on the back of a bus, it was everywhere. Not only did TV and movies bring us heartwarming stories of perfection (diamond commercials, love stories ending in an "I do," and all that jazz), they also bombarded us with not-so-perfect times. The times when engagement was a problem, not a promise. It was usually in the form of a comedy's hearty laugh at the woman's expense or a drama that ended with a pile of Kleenex on your living room floor.

The phenomenon of the missing ring was even happening when I turned off the TV—like during weekend gossip fests with friends over coffee. I'd barely have blown the foam off my cappuccino when it would begin. With the good ("Did you hear so-and-so got engaged?") came the bad ("Did you hear so-and-so still isn't engaged?"). I thought to myself, "Maybe I'm onto something. Does every couple go through this transition?"

I sparked conversations with others about their experiences, and found this waiting time . . . this frustration . . . this argh factor . . . was a relationship passage in itself. It wasn't a fear of general relationship commitment (the generic commitment phobia) because the couples it plagues have the commitment thing down pat—their relationships have seen several pages of the calendar flipped. No, this was different. I decided to give it a name. Say hello to "pre-engagement limbo."

When it's you who's going through this relationship standstill, you can't help but feel like you're the only one. All you can think of is how the engagement party Evites are filling up your inbox. You don't exactly want to announce to the girls over brunch that your long-term boyfriend doesn't want to be your long-term husband. Imagine the looks of pity! And the secret thoughts of "What's wrong with her?" It would only make you feel more vulnerable. So it's sealed lips and tell-nothing smiles. The truth is, the woman with the latte and scone at the next table might be going through the same thing. The hush-hush leads to another missed opportunity for chick bonding.

Women frustrated with the pace of their relationship say they also feel embarrassed and rejected by their partner's hesitancy. Surprisingly, hesitancy doesn't necessarily mean rejection. In most cases, the reason a man might dodge the *M*-word has little to do with his girlfriend and instead has a lot to do with his own personal struggle and individual pace. Discomfort with change, ideals of perfection, fear of the unknown, and even wondering if Cindy Crawford is looking for him right now can all keep a guy frozen at the knee.

MY OWN CASE OF LIMBO

I was in a relationship with a man who initially had trouble sorting out his own feelings about getting engaged. I learned a lot from this man. He's now my husband.

While we were dating, I was talking with a therapist once a week for a couple of months. I needed to figure it all out. Was I in a dead-end relationship? Should I end it and move on or stick it out for the light at the end of the tunnel (maybe the sparkle of a diamond)? Each week I found myself asking her for a translation of my boyfriend's process, as if she could read the mind of someone she had never met. I wanted a crystal ball, a prediction about how everything would turn out. Were we going to end up together? Was he just going through "stuff"? Was it a simple case of his cold feet or something more?

I vented my frustration to a few of my closest friends, and initially swore them to secrecy—an adult pinky swear that my "shame" wouldn't get out. I couldn't bear the thought of people wondering if I was part of a couple in the midst of a standoff. Would they think something was wrong with me or with my relationship?

When people asked me the question I *didn't* want to be asked, "When are you two going to get married?" I would hold my chin up high, stand up straight, and try to fool them all by responding, "What's the rush?" What I really wanted to scream was, "It's none of your business!" It always amazes me that such a personal question is asked so casually and so often. How was your day? When are you getting married? What's for dinner?

I wanted to understand. I needed more insight into what was actually happening with my relationship. At the time, my boyfriend couldn't give me answers to my questions because he had his own conflicting feelings. So I began my quest for information about the "whys" of the "why nots" of proposing. During my search, I found studies and statistics about how much more difficult it is for men to commit to marriage than it is for women. Miss Misery might love company, but the numbers and case studies didn't seem to help me. I still felt alone.

After leaving the self-help section of the bookstore empty-handed again, I decided it was time to cross the line. The only way to do that—talk to the boys. So I called my closest friends' husbands for a man's perspective. I wanted their thoughts on my situation and to find out whether they were afraid to pop their own question to their brides. When did Boys Chase the Girls turn into No Girls Allowed? What makes men tick? Or shall I say, what makes their clocks stop?

Most responded by exclaiming, "Are you kidding? Of course I was afraid to get engaged!" They seemed eager to delve into the past and give me the tell-alls about their experiences. Finally, I was getting honest answers to my questions! These chats helped me begin to understand my own partner. The stories I heard eventually enabled me to talk to my boyfriend about his feelings without taking his comments too personally or defensively. We were able to talk together, transforming what was once so frustrating into one of the richest growing experiences of our relationship.

Considering how helpful it was to hear from other couples also stuck in pre-engagement limbo, I knew this was a topic that needed to get out in the open. The paper I wrote in the spring of 2003 during grad school, "Let's Hear It from the Men: The Word on Getting Married," also seemed to spark a bit of interest on the matter. I became inspired to press on.

I continued my research, probing with questions no one had dared to ask:

"What influences you the most to get engaged?"
"How does it feel when friends ask what's taking so long?"
"Why is it so difficult to talk about the *M*-word?"

I conducted interviews. I distributed surveys. Realizing just how differently women and men approach this step in their lives, I wanted women to see that the door to the chapel doesn't always open easily and getting to the altar isn't always a breeze. I was eager to share what I learned and to guide others through their own pre-engagement stage. To much fanfare, I launched the Web site HisColdFeet.com in February 2005, and started on this journey that led to the book you now hold in your hand.

I remember when a friend read an early draft of my book proposal. After reading a section about how pre-engagement limbo affects women emotionally, she gave me a little feedback that began with the question, "Are you sure women are going to want to read about themselves in this light? You describe how women become consumed with wanting to get engaged." She thought I should leave that part out.

But that's exactly what's been happening. "That part" has been left out of the culture on engagement. The part about how women feel rejected, frustrated, devalued. Leaving it out only makes women feel more confused and alone. She was wrong about another aspect. These women I speak of aren't needy or weak. On the contrary, they're strong, and they know what they want. They're from all walks of life: They run finance departments of major corporations; they're doctors, artists, teachers. It can happen to anyone—regardless of age, station, or career choice.

Within the pages of *His Cold Feet,* you'll read stories from amazing women and men who share their experiences with the determination to let others know they aren't alone. You'll find tips and exercises to help you manage your own pre-engagement limbo and effectively communicate with your partner about that walk down the aisle. Featured are survey results, interview excerpts, and frequently asked questions I've run into along the way.

While I was working on this book, I interviewed my former graduate school professor Judye Hess, Ph.D., for her take on the matter. A psychologist in the Bay Area, Dr. Hess taught my favorite graduate course on couples therapy. Throughout *His Cold Feet,* she offers helpful hints and valuable insight in her "Notes from the Professor" sections.

If you acknowledge pre-engagement limbo as a normal relationship stage that most couples encounter, you won't be surprised when it shows up on your doorstep. You'll be able to grasp it and get through it, rather than let it move in and take over.

Most importantly, when it comes to talking about the *M*-word, getting engaged, and planning the wedding, it's helpful to know that women and men are programmed differently. Understanding each other's perspective about that walk down the aisle is the essential ingredient needed to get you through the pre-engagement passage. I hope *His Cold Feet* helps you manage pre-engagement limbo together as a couple, guiding you toward the same goal of a happily-ever-after.

1

The Eternal Question: When Are You Getting Married?

It looks as simple as boy meets
girl, girl lights up boy's life,
boy can't imagine life without
her, boy tells her he wants to be
with her forever, proposes,
and girl says yes. Well, it's not.

—DIANA, 30

So, you've finally found The One. You've been dating for a while, and you're ready to move your relationship to the next level. And you're probably thinking the path to that level is adorned with pew bows and a flower girl leading the way. You're ready to get engaged. However, the guy you're counting on to pop the question isn't. Ain't love grand?

To sum it up: You want to tie the knot; he wants to talk about it later. And when you think about his turtle's pace, all you can do is muster up more questions. "More time?" "Talk about it later?" "Why is this happening?" "Where's the surprise proposal?" "Where's the romance?"

Although we grow up seeing marriage proposals as fairy tales, it might just be that before Prince Charming gets down on one knee, he first has to slay the dragon. That big, scaly, nasty monster appropriately named Jitters. For some, this feat is a necessary evil before he can rescue the princess. When the tale of a dreamy marriage proposal goes from fact to fiction, you feel just as ripped off as you did when you found out the real story behind the Tooth Fairy. Welcome to pre-engagement limbo.

PRE-ENGAGEMENT LIMBO, n.: The common relationship dynamic when a woman is ready to get married before her long-term boyfriend. Symptoms:

- You start to track friends' engagements like a hawk.
- You develop a mailman phobia. You know that if another wedding invitation shows up in the mailbox, another bickering session with your beau is inevitable.
- You start to feel rejected and question your own self-worth.
- Your stomach aches when you think about your future: "Will I always be just a bridesmaid?"
- You're one calendar page away from another ringless Valentine's Day.
- You realize that there's one game that you don't particularly like playing: the waiting game.

> When I was ready to get engaged before my boyfriend,
> I felt self-doubt and loathing. I thought I wasn't
> good enough.
>
> —TANYA, 37

When you want to get engaged and your boyfriend isn't ready, it's obvious that you both want two different things. The power struggle lands you in a boxing ring instead of with a ring box. The pushing and pulling, the jibs and jabs, bobbing and weaving—it becomes an emotional roller coaster that leaves you exhausted and feeling like you're taking two steps forward while he's standing still or worse . . . stepping backward. The distance between you grows, and you find yourself at wit's end.

To top it off, you're dodging the most uninvited question of all time, "When are you two getting married?" A question that, if you really think about it, is quite ridiculous. It makes you wonder about the people who ask it. Did they misplace their invitation? Are they concerned you're keeping the date secret? It would stand to reason that if you knew when you were getting married, they probably would have gotten a save-the-date card already, yes? So questions like these only push you further and further away from happiness, and closer to the edge.

To be fair, these questions can be good conversation starters; they break the ice and are probably asked merely out of curiosity. Some (usually your older relatives) ask because they genuinely don't want to see you stuck in a nowhere relationship, and they believe it's up to them to bring your attention to this possibility (as if you were sitting in the dark until they flipped on the light for you). And yes, sometimes the town gossip asks just to be nosy. Even though no one means to hurt your feelings, and people mean no harm by asking if they should start dress-shopping for your big day, it stings to be on the receiving end of these innocent quips. In short, they only make your engagement itch turn into more of an allergic reaction.

A TYPICAL SCENE

You go home for your cousin's wedding, and at the conclusion of the ceremony Great-Aunt Edith puts her arm around you and asks, "When is it going to be your turn?" Along with this jarring question come words of advice: "You're not getting any younger, you know." Gee, thanks, Aunt Edith. Your mind starts spinning and your engine starts to rev. Uncle Charlie chimes in: "Is your generation familiar with the phrase 'Why buy the cow if you can get the milk for free'?" Your thoughts: "That's funny. I didn't see my name on the program as this evening's entertainment."

By the time dinner is served, you've found out that half the guests are "concerned." Your mother calmly explains, "We're just worried about you, honey." She makes it sound like you have a weird addiction or a rash or an appalling sense of fashion, instead of a boyfriend who isn't jumping at the chance to be your husband.

Your heart's racing at this point; your imagination runs wild. You picture tables 5 and 10 placing bets on whether he'll ever propose. There's nowhere to hide. You even catch your nana's friends chatting in the ladies' room, tossing around phrases like "oh, the poor thing," "and she has such a pretty face," and "what a shame."

More panic. You think everyone is convinced you'll be an old maid. Just as your beau dreads it when you bring up the E-word (you know, the one that rhymes with enragement), you've also started to dread it when other people approach the subject. Once you've been drilled with "When are you two getting married?" you start to feel like something's supposed to be happening in your relationship that isn't. Why else would everyone under the sun be wondering about it? If things were great, wouldn't they leave you be?

Finally the fiasco comes to an end, and you're relieved you made it through your cousin's wedding weekend. To further escape, you actually don't mind going back to work on Monday. It'll be good to get your mind off things relating to love, marriage, and your ring size.

On your way up to the fourth-floor conference room, you run into a coworker in the elevator. Making small talk about the weekend, you tell her you went to a wedding. Innocent small talk quickly transforms into uninvited chitchat when she asks, "Speaking of weddings, when are you and your boyfriend going to get a move on? Haven't you been together a few years now?" The elevator stops. As she gets off on her floor, you think to yourself, "What did I ever do to her?"

POP GOES THE QUESTION

When I was in limbo with my boyfriend (now hubby), I added "our relationship" to the list of topics to avoid at a dinner party. But no matter how hard I tried, I couldn't get away from it. I'm surprised our life together wasn't the cover story of *People,* everyone seemed to be so interested. Brangelina had nothing on us!

Much to my surprise, sometimes even total strangers would ask about my relationship. For instance, we were visiting family in New Haven, Connecticut, and took a boat ride with about twenty other people around the Long Island Sound. Our very animated captain was pointing out landmark after landmark, telling joke after joke, and when making a side reference to something, he asked me, "How long have you two been married?" Since that ship hadn't set sail yet, I corrected him with, "We're actually not married, just dating." He acted shocked, asking, "Why not?" Then my little cousin shouted out from the back of the boat, "He's got commitment issues!" I swear I think these words actually echoed loudly enough across the water for everyone on Long Island to hear. But secretly, I was happy someone asked about marriage. Someone besides me.

We tend to think there's a big difference between being asked about our potential upcoming nuptials when the boyfriend is within earshot, compared to when he's not. When he's there, we actually feel it makes all the difference in the world. Now he'll see that it's not just you who thinks it's time, but the captain in New Haven agrees! That'll get him thinking, right? You believe there's now more credence to your complaints. After all, you have a cheering section behind you.

As much as we want to believe this is the push he needs, in reality his being around to endure the questions really has little to no effect. Sure, it may give him a taste of what you're up against. It might even make him feel bad about not proposing yet. But it certainly won't make him dart to the jeweler just because Aunt Edith and Uncle Charlie think he should.

THE ENGAGEMENT ITCH

Ever wonder what it would be like if no one questioned the whens and whats of your pre-engaged status? Would the engagement itch ease up a bit? Would you not feel as rushed to take the plunge? This gets me thinking about how we're influenced by the questions people ask and by what others are doing.

We're all guilty of it—being influenced by our surroundings. Why else would the latest and greatest worn and driven by the bold and beautiful of Hollywood pique our interest? Since we're all slightly competitive by nature, tracking our lives becomes a sort of game—a competition against everyone else our age. Even with things like where we are in our relationship. It might not be about what *others* are doing, but how we interpret the questions we're asked about what *we're* doing: "Where's the ring?" "What about kids?" "Why do you think he hasn't proposed?" We take these as hints. They become ways to calculate if we're on track with the other players in our age category.

Although we both deal with pressures of measuring up, men and women are triggered and influenced by different things. Just think of prime-time TV. You wouldn't see a beer or men's deodorant ad during a *Desperate Housewives* episode, or an Overstock .com or Cover Girl commercial during an NCAA basketball game.

Remember how as young girls we wanted to have what our friends had? I can't even count how many times I whined growing up, "But, Mom, everyone has them!" Whether I was complaining about the latest Guess jeans or pierced ears, I wanted to be like Them. The girls who were too cool for school. Besides, it was cute for us little ladies to call our BFF Sunday night to plan our matching outfits for the week. On the flip side, if my brother ever showed up to class dressed identically to his best friend, he would have been horrified.

Men do have their own things. They compare. They may not be on the lookout for what everyone who's anyone is wearing this fall, but when it comes down to a high-level job, a big salary, or doing something cool (like actually making it as a rock star), guys can relate. For instance, I have a friend who pushes himself extra hard to reach his career goals after hearing so-and-so hit it big in real estate or what's-his-name just bought a flat-screen TV.

Even though we try our best to be happy with what we've got, sometimes we get tempted to want what other people have. Whether it's clothes, cars, jobs, or houses, the grass is always greener. So, does the same go for life passages? Maybe it's only natural for us to want to have the fairy-tale love affair that everyone around us seems to be enjoying. Not to mention the two-carat that your neighbor's flashing when she goes to get the mail. I bet wedding invites in her mailbox don't cast a shadow over it.

And nothing's more obvious than when things happen in groups—especially when you aren't part of that group. Doesn't it seem that everyone you know got married within a few years of each other? Or bought a house? Or had a baby? For a while there, I could have bought four wedding gifts on one receipt. When I went to pick out a baby shower gift, I was able to say, "I'll take three." Are we constantly just trying to keep up?

TAMING YOUR LITTLE GREEN MONSTER

When dishing out advice on how to deal and not feel rushed when all your friends are getting engaged, I say don't compare. I know this isn't an easy task. It almost sounds foreign, since for our entire lives we've been making comparisons and being compared. In the classroom, we were compared to our peers. On the playing field, it was our teammates. At a job interview, we need to beat out the other applicants. Were we basically trained under the conditions of being evaluated, compared, and judged? Maybe this is why we desire to feel accepted, ultimately by the boyfriend who proves you're all he wants—you're better than all the others—by asking, "Will you marry me?"

It might take some time before you're no longer worrying about whether your engagement time frame is in line with your younger sister's. But there are ways to bring yourself out of the frenzy and back down to earth.

Catch yourself when you're comparing and nip it in the bud. Don't get wrapped up in what other people have going on. Your friend with the newly shined diamond on her ring finger and her fiancé might be in a different place than you and your boyfriend. Remember that no two relationships are alike. Try to keep your focus on your own life.

When your social calendar is full of other people's nuptials and you're sure you'll be bombarded with "Why not you?" the second you get to the reception, take your own steps not to let these queries get you worked up. Believe it or not, your honest reactions to these questions can give you a little insight into your true feelings. If the woman who initially claims that everything is just dandy with her relationship status gets riled up when someone asks, "When are you going to get married?" that means something. There's information there. These questions bother us because they're pushing a button. A button that leads to a part in our relationship that isn't completely satisfying us.

A LITTLE WORKOUT SESSION

Try this exercise to help you understand your reactions to being asked, "When are you getting married?" Instead of jogging your mind for the perfect sarcastic comeback zing, focus on the following cues:

- How do you feel emotionally (overwhelmed, neutral, anxious)?
- What are your thoughts ("He better propose by my birthday," "He better have a good reason for waiting this out," etc.)?
- What does your body feel like physically (tense, awake, drained)?

Your triggers provide information that something's going on that you need to address. If you're dodging under your desk when you hear a coworker ask "when"—then this might be a good indication you need to get more in touch with how you feel about your relationship. Try chatting with your guy, and if you're not ready for that yet, how about turning to a friend? Or do a little journaling. Observing your reactions will bring you closer to your feelings. Listen to them.

WHEN IT RAINS, IT POURS

When you think about it, it's kind of shocking that personal questions about our love life and home life seem to be up for grabs by anyone. They fly around birthday parties, weddings, baby showers, the office, and even the sauna. I'm not joking. The sauna.

I remember it like it was yesterday. One afternoon I was in the sauna, basking in the quiet and warmth after a workout. Suddenly my personal space was invaded, and this woman next to me asked me about kids. When was I going to have them, she wanted to know. The quiet was gone, and the warmth had now turned up a notch to an unbearable level. (Or was it just me?) Why was she bothering me about this? I had never even met this curious woman before. It's not like she was going to be their grandmother, so why did she care?

When I asked others whether they were guilty of showering people they know with "When are you going to get married?" or "When are you going to have kids?" some were and some weren't. Most said that if they did ask, it was simply a conversation starter or just a case of the Curious Cat.

Sometimes I'm just curious about what's going on in their relationship. Other times I ask so I can compare my relationship to theirs. In my head I'm doing the math— they've been together for a year and moved in together six months ago. And I've been dating my boyfriend for two and a half years and we're not even living together yet. Then I wonder, am I behind on this? I end up feeling bad about it, but that doesn't stop me

from asking someone else when they think
they'll get engaged. —STEPHANIE, 28

But in some cases it was clear skies ahead. Not a drop in sight. There are no questions, just acceptance.

I would never ask someone about when they're going
to get engaged because I thought it was absolutely
painful when someone asked me. I dealt with the questions
for five years. I never want to make someone
feel uncomfortable. —JAMIE, 34

HOW TO STAY DRY

If it's not one stage, it's another. Life is full of situations that draw people's curiosity. "When are you (insert life decision here—getting engaged, having children, buying a new house, retiring)?" Everyone wants to pick apart life.

After getting married, Jamie and Matt thought they were in the clear. Then, after celebrating their second anniversary, they were inundated with questions about when they were going to have kids. They just couldn't catch a break!

You probably fantasize about making spicy comebacks to the question "When are you going to get engaged?" Something like "When are you going to start coloring your hair to cover that gray?" Or maybe you want to trap the questioner in a corner and spill your guts out about your hopes, dreams, and fears. Too much honesty when people ask how you are usually will stop them from ever asking again. But you're too classy for any of this. You know that throwing out a dig or freaking them out with a sob story isn't the answer. Being able to cope gracefully when someone is in your business is a helpful trait throughout life—not just during pre-engagement limbo.

As we get older, we get even more secure with ourselves. We decide that we don't need to answer anything from anyone if it makes us uncomfortable. In an attempt to shoo off unwanted inquiring minds, one day we'll respond more honestly than in the past. Honesty, although the best policy, is not always the sweetest. With more years comes less sugar. I heard someone ask my friend's dad, "Do you think you'll retire soon?" His snappy reply: "Why, do you think I'm old or something? What's the matter with you?"

I'm not a fan of e-mail chains, but there was one I was glad didn't make it to my trash folder. It was a list of necessary things in life and tips on handling different situations. Right beneath the importance of every woman having a little black dress was a tip on what to do when you're asked a question you don't want to answer. The advice was to respond with "What makes you ask?" When you don't feel like talking, turn things around and let the other person do the talking. Your inquisitive neighbor asks, "When are you two getting married?" You simply reply, "What makes you ask?" Conversation over.

If answering a question with a question isn't your style, there's another way of dealing with the pre-prenuptial series of inquiries. Think of these questions for what they are—conversation pieces. (Of course, this depends on who's asking. If your nana asks, there may be an undertone of how she wants to see you married with kids.) How about turning "What's she hinting at?" into "She's trying to make conversation"? When you're in limbo and you don't know the answers, all the questions can be a drag. But know that no one means to intentionally hurt you.

If you really want to dodge the question, ask them something about themselves to get their mind off you. Just as much as people love getting the 411, they love talking about themselves (maybe even more so). Something like "What's been going on with you?" or "Where did you find that fabulous suit?" is sure to get them rolling. They'll forget what they asked you in the first place.

FAQ

Question: I'm going home for a family event, and I just know everyone's going to drill me about when my boyfriend and I are going to get engaged. This is very sensitive, and I know I'm only going to get upset. How do I get through this?

Answer: It's great you're preparing yourself for the En-gagement Inquisition. No matter what stage in life we are in, people will be asking about it. Our society thinks about life passages in terms of steps. Remember, when you graduated, you weren't out of school for a month before people started asking, "So what are your plans?" "Did you get a job yet?" Now you've got the long-term boyfriend, and everyone wants to know what's next. I know this is a sensitive time for you right now, but the way to deal is to try not to take these questions personally. And don't feel like you have to engage in talking about your personal life if that's not what you want to do. A quick reply like "We're

not sure, but we'll let you know when we decide" should
do the trick.

> [People] asking didn't help the situation. It made us feel that
> we were supposed to be engaged already. I took people's
> questions to mean "What's wrong with him, what's
> wrong with you, and what's wrong with your
> relationship?" —LISA, 33

WHEN HE'S CAUGHT IN THE DOWNPOUR

It's more often that women take the brunt of the questions on
where the relationship stands. (Just look below at how little guys
have to say about this one.) But when men have to dodge one
here and there, some get defensive, while others laugh it off. Ask
a guy, "So when are you getting married?" and in the best-case
scenario, he hears, "Blah blah blah." In the worst-case scenario
he hears, "What's wrong with you? How come you haven't proposed yet?" His defensiveness might even affect you by his
adding a few months to the proposal date. Why? Because the last
thing guys want to do is conform. When they propose, it's going
to be a decision they make on their own, and not because it's the
"in" thing to do.

> The heat got turned up for me when our mutual friends
> who started dating after us got married before us. I said
> to my buddy, "Yeah, man, the kitchen just got cooler for you
> and a lot hotter for me." That was the only time when it
> got really tough [in my relationship]. When people would ask
> us when we were going to get married, it was a lot harder

for my girlfriend. She did a tremendous job at not putting it back at me. But toward the end, something would come up and the issue would bubble up and out of nowhere she'd start asking me the questions. —RYAN, 34

• • •

The average guy doesn't have pressure to get married [from other people]. The only pressure he feels is from the woman he's dating. He feels the pressure *NOT* to get married from his buddies. Because if he falls, they're going to have to fall. —JACK, 30

TONGUE-TIED

When I'm asked a question that catches me off guard or makes me uncomfortable, I get the same feeling I used to get when a teacher would call on me when I hadn't read the day's assignment. I get stuck and flub up my words . . . er . . . um . . . er . . . ah . . . Then, four hours later, I replay over and over what I wish I had said. Why didn't I just say this or that?! Oh, yes, I was brilliant— but only after the conversation was over.

Whether it's a coworker who confronts you out of the blue at a staff meeting, or your neighbor who wants the latest on your love life, we all get stuck on how to respond when we're caught off guard. Why? Because that's what being surprised does. Should it be any different than when you were completely stunned at your Sweet Sixteen surprise party? You opened the door, everyone screamed "Surprise!" and you just stood there. Mouth open. Nothing coming out.

When the surprise isn't for a birthday (in this case, it's a pity party), we tend to get stuck and later obsess over how we wish we had responded. Familiar with the phrase "Look before you leap"? Well, the same goes here. Don't jump to respond if that's not what you want to do. It's okay to take some time to put your thoughts together before answering. It's when we make a move too quickly that we feel uncomfortable and we second-guess our actions later. Taking a moment to pause before firing a response will help put you at ease.

When questions affect us, we learn about our sensitivities. Just as we dodge people that don't make us feel good, we try to dodge questions that do the same. Sometimes taking a look at the questions that sting helps us recognize the issues in our life we need to explore and improve.

ARE ANY TWO BUTTONS ALIKE?

People are constantly grilling me about when
I'm getting married. You have to think about what's
good for you. —STEPHANIE, 28

So much of what happens (and is going to happen) for the couple in pre-engagement limbo is individual. And so are the things that push our buttons. This is the case for everything life throws at us.

For instance, I called a friend of mine to wish her a happy birthday. While I was on the phone with her, she received a bouquet of roses from her husband. I asked what they were going to do tonight. She responded with "Nothing, he's in Newport for a guys' weekend." I was stunned. She continued, "Yeah, they couldn't pin down a weekend—this was the only available one."

She was totally cool with that. I, on the other hand, would have had a big problem. I just know I would. My mind would become preoccupied with thoughts like "What, am I not as important as the guys?" or "I always plan something special for his birthday. How could he blow mine off?" or "Guy weekend—shmy weekend."

I hung up the phone and thought, "Wow! We really all do have our own individual triggers." The week before, she was telling me how she couldn't believe that my hubby and I were meeting an ex-girlfriend of his for lunch. Her words: "What do you mean you're all going out?" But this wasn't my trigger. This didn't bug me.

We all have our own buttons. But what bothers a dear friend may not bother you. And vice versa. When your hot topic gets approached (why you're with a guy who hasn't proposed), don't be easily influenced. Look inward. What do you think?

Just as we discover what triggers our friends, we need to get to know our partners and what sets them off. There's no right or wrong to our soft spots. Although "treat others as you would want to be treated" is true, in this case, a slight modification might work better. Treat your partner as you know he would like to be treated.

Throughout this book you'll discover techniques to identify your style and his, handy tricks of the trade when dealing with some of the pre-engagement limbo themes. First, let's take a look at what causes hot feet.

2

Her Hot Feet:
It's Time We Got Engaged

He would ask if it was him that I
wanted, or if it was a wedding
I was excited about.
—DIANA, 30

When my friend Amy and I were having dinner one night, she relived the emotional roller coaster she had been on for the last few months. She was in a long-term relationship and not sure where it was headed. Every time she brought up the subject of marriage with her boyfriend, the conversation skidded to a halt as if someone had pulled an imaginary emergency brake. I was inundated with her questions. What was he waiting for? Would he ever propose? Instead of even attempting answers, I found myself asking her one of my own. "Why do you want to get engaged right now?"

Instead of an answer, I got a priceless look that came with its own sound effect: "Duh." After a long dumbfounded pause, she finally spoke. "You're kidding, right? Of course you know why."

For some of us, "just because" is good enough. When I was waiting for a proposal of my own, I don't think I ever took the time to think about what it was I wanted so badly and why I wanted it at that particular time. What was my "just because"?

I remember a therapy session when I couldn't stop talking. I took up the entire fifty minutes ranting and raving about my relationship that seemed destined for eternal limbo. Then my therapist interrupted to ask why I wanted to get engaged. I paused and looked at her blankly. Was this a rhetorical question? I looked at her looking at me with this expectant expression on her face. So I rambled off a checklist of my boyfriend's loving qualities, talked about how he was my best friend, and how he was the first man I ever wanted to marry. With a little attitude in my voice, I summed it up with "I love him and want to spend my life with him." (Okay, she can stop staring at me now.)

Finally, my therapist realized she wasn't going to get what she was looking for, so she asked a different question. Actually it was the same question, just rephrased. "So why do you want to get married at this point in your relationship?" I guess she was pointing out that you could be in love and not want to get married, or at least you could be in love and not want to get married right now. I sat and thought. Then she said, "Time's up." Something for me to ponder on the ride home.

Up until that moment, I was so busy analyzing why he wasn't jumping up and yelling "hooray" whenever I mentioned "engagement" that I never took the time to figure out why it was so important for me to get engaged at this point in our relationship. It was as if I were doing his work but none of my own.

CAN "JUST BECAUSE" BECOME
"JUST MARRIED"?

When Amy asked her boyfriend about getting engaged, he usually countered with "What's your rush?" Not only did this make her want to jump up and scream, but it also left her quiet and stumped. Her response became "Just because." All of her friends were getting married, and she felt like they were passing her. A common concern, yet not something you want to look someone in the eye and actually admit you're thinking. She wanted to hide from societal influences, but sticking your head in the sand isn't always an option. Amy was searching for reasons why she wanted to announce an engagement (right now) while simultaneously keeping the wolves at bay (questioning friends and family). Sometimes we need to wash away all the clutter that prevents us from reaching our place of reason. Not an easy task, but an important one.

Perhaps among girlfriends there is an unspoken understanding that we know exactly why each of us wants a proposal when we want it. Whenever I speed-dialed one of the girls for the hundredth time to vent about my boyfriend dragging his feet, no one questioned my urgency. It was like they had all been through it. They just . . . knew. I did get the occasional "just enjoy your relationship the way it is now" response, which was truly annoying. As if it were a simple recipe for happiness: Just add patience and stir.

A guy friend of mine told me it all boils down to Marisa Tomei's character in *My Cousin Vinny*. In a thick Brooklyn accent, she explains why she wants to set a date: "My biological clock is ticking like this," while stamping her foot on the ground. My friend suggested that since biological clocks just aren't a worry for men, where's the rush? I didn't buy it. Lots of guys talk about wanting to be young parents, rolling around in the backyard after tossing the ball, coaching their Little League All-Stars for the big game. They want all this without having to stay in bed for days afterward, loading up on aspirin and heating pads. Granted, their biological clocks tick a lot more slowly than women's, but they're ticking.

> Men don't have the biological clock pushing them to think differently. The woman wants kids, and she has a time frame on that. Men don't have anything similar, so they don't know what it's like. —SETH, 36

This friend also had tales of caveman days, when men were hunters and women were nesters. Today's woman has traded in her cave for a nice two-car-garage Tudor, while today's man still attempts to feed his need to hunt—and this time his prey is women. An interesting twist to the familiar caveman theories, but the story seemed more complicated than that. Fred Flintstone didn't have a problem settling down with Wilma. Besides, cavemen and cavewomen didn't have Hollywood whispering in their ears or diamond commercials pulling on their heartstrings in an attempt to open their purse strings. It has to be more than primal instinct.

I started to explore why I wanted to get engaged when I did, and I have to admit that some issues came up I wasn't proud to call my own. When I looked around, there was pressure everywhere: questioning family members, a summer calendar booked with weddings, TV show season finales. (Will Ross and Rachel tie the knot?) Could all this peripheral stuff actually affect me?

I asked other unengaged women why they were in such a rush. The ladies started talking, and soon I learned of a common ingredient—we want to marry our boyfriends because we can't picture our world without them. We've got the unconditional true love, respect, admiration, a best friendship, etc. This makes sense. Now combine that with a synthetic mixture chock-full of preservatives: pressures from family and friends, societal messages, and beliefs about time frames. All of a sudden, the temperature gets turned up and this pot's about to boil. It's important to be aware of all these reasons, so you can see what actually contributes to your engagement itch.

Even though I had my follow-the-crowd moments as a young woman, I always thought I grew into a strong, hear-me-roar woman. I wasn't influenced by anyone else's schedule or pressure. Well, I was wrong. When friends with shorter relationships than mine began sending out save-the-date cards, I started to question why we weren't flipping through invitation books and catering menus. I wondered what was wrong with us.

There are things about ourselves we're always judging. Do I look fat in these Diesels? Does this kitten heel make my calves look big? Should I whiten my teeth? But when we look at our reasons for wanting to get engaged we're talking about what's going on inside. How do we figure out what our true motivations really are?

A friend tossed a little Zen philosophy my way. She told me not to judge my reasons but to simply be aware of them. Only then would I progress on my journey to realize the "deeper meaning."

That sounded impressive (and so California!). I definitely wanted to progress on my journey. I shared this "enlightenment" with a yogi friend. He explained in plain English that usually there is a deeper meaning behind most things we want, including an immediate engagement. He related it to the way many people like to have material possessions to make up for something they may be lacking in another part of their lives. Now this was registering with me, and slowly the concept started to come together.

If we can get a new pair of Manolo Blahniks or another Prada bag, we can distract ourselves from problems. (No wonder it's called Retail Therapy!) Is it possible we could be doing the same with an engagement ring, just on a larger scale? If that's it, then the first step must be simply to recognize the possibility that it exists without judging ourselves, and just admit that it may be part of human nature. We instinctually seek pleasure, avoid pain, and fill voids in our lives the best way we can. Is it possible that a diamond ring might just be an expensive Band-Aid to help us feel better about ourselves and more secure? Showing the world that yes, we are loved.

Once we understand why we want some of the things we crave, we truly get to know ourselves better. Our desire to get engaged can be for many reasons—we love this person and we want our lives to start together right now; we just got another wedding invitation in the mail; we want security; and on and on. Regardless of what contributes to the *right now* factor, ultimately this awareness helps us get in better touch with ourselves.

WHERE THE HELL IS MARS?

I remember those talks with my beau about getting engaged that made me feel as though we were on completely different planets. These conversations circled for hours. It boggles men's minds why women spend so much time fixated on getting engaged, while women can't understand why men spend so much time avoiding it. Even with all the pushing and pulling in this fierce game of tug-of-war, there's something we all have in common after all. By recognizing it, everyone may be able to see eye-to-eye. It's P-R-E-S-S-U-R-E.

Whether it's what you say to yourself, what others say to you, or the silent screaming from the covers of bridal magazines, both women and men are managing the pressure to get married. And the problem is that this pressure forces couples in opposite directions. It pulls women toward marriage and pushes men away from it. It takes over like a tornado leaving a couple in a cycle of relationship rut, dealing with misunderstanding after misunderstanding. But all along they're simply both struggling with the same problem. If they try to relate to one another in terms of this weight they share, it can make a difference in how they interpret what each other is saying. The weight will be easier to carry if they share the load.

"When are you two going to get married?" "What's taking so long?" "Do you think he'll ever propose?" These questions make a woman feel her relationship isn't where it's supposed to be ("What's wrong with me?") and pushes her to want to start typing up a guest list even faster. These same questions make a man want to add six months to the proposal because he's attached to wanting to propose on his own terms ("Get off my back!"). Not to get Freudian here, but this may even resemble rebelliousness, since he definitely doesn't want to feel like he's being told what to do. His mother did that.

This reminds me of a game I played with the cute boy in elementary school. I would say let's go left, and he would go right. I would say let's run, and he would walk very slowly. Sometimes I feel life has come full circle, and we're back in kindergarten playing the same way. But at least the boys have stopped pulling our hair!

RUNNERS, TAKE YOUR MARK

I imagined getting in touch with my inner feelings about engagement during some life-changing epiphany. Some major event would occur, making it all crystal clear. A voice in my head would say, "That's it!" Gongs would sound. Lights would flash. My life would be different from then on.

As it turned out, there was a ringing. But it was just the phone. My nana called me. She told me to hurry up and plan a wedding already, because she wanted a reason to go on a diet and shop for a dress. I realized at that silly moment how much I wanted to get engaged. Not exactly a pivotal point in time, but an epiphany of some sort. Right then I found myself storming around our house and actually starting a fight with my boyfriend. I was hitting him over the head with a pillow while screeching, "What are you waiting for, what is taking you so long, my nana wants a dress, what is your problem?!" And there it was. I had reached my low point. As they say, the feelings you don't deal with will come up sooner or later to bite ya.

When a (sincere) boyfriend says, "I love you, but I don't want to get engaged right now," he isn't lying. He does love his girlfriend, but he's bogged down with a slew of messages from society, his friends, and even the comedian who cracked jokes about marriage all night (not a good show to see when you're in limbo). Just the notion of getting a "hall pass" from his wife is enough to make anyone want to stay single. Typically, women and men are exposed to influences but react in different ways.

Voicing "I want to get married, and my long-term boyfriend is still unsure if he wants to marry me" makes a woman feel utterly embarrassed, not to mention weak. If we lay down the statistics, we see there's nothing to feel weak about. Vegas bookmakers would say the odds are high that a woman will want to tie the knot before her guy.

WHAT YOU SAID

One hundred and sixteen people were asked: Women tend to feel ready to get engaged before men feel ready to propose, true or false?

89 percent: true
11 percent: false

For women, perhaps it's once you hit the one-year mark that you know if you're taking the relationship down the aisle or not. You decide that the direction's there. And you aren't straying from the path. For men, it's a little more difficult. Right when they're about to go in one direction, they get distracted at an intersection and think about going another way. We may obsess about getting engaged, but men obsess over where each path may take them. This is the beginning of their wrestling match with "If I choose marriage, I'll be giving up path a, b, and c . . . what if I make a mistake?" (More on what men are thinking in chapter 4.)

I heard from a twenty-two-year-old woman who wrote that she wanted to get married and her boyfriend wasn't ready. My initial reaction was, she's only in her early twenties—how does she know she wants to get married? Then I reflected back to when I was her age. The days when after a fabulous first date I'd call my best friend to say, "I think I just met my husband." Then it could be after Date #3 or even after a one-year relationship when I'd realize, "Nah, that wasn't him." So my search would continue.

Bad breakups and awful first dates are exhausting. Once a

woman finds the potential husband-to-be, regardless of where she is in life, she's probably ready to step it up to tie the knot after about a year or so of dating. Most guys feel differently. They don't look at dating as exhausting. (Expensive, maybe, but not exhausting.) To quote one guy, "It's fun to be back on the market."

I'm now in my early thirties, and I still get two different dating reports from men and women my age. Women friends share stories that sound like nightmares. Guys give reports with high fives.

I mentioned earlier that women want to get married because of how much they love their boyfriends, but there are some more reasons too. To quote a few:

I want to start having kids like all my friends.

—VICKI, 38

• • •

I always thought I'd be married by now.

—RANDI, 33

• • •

We're the only couple out of our group of friends
not married yet. —JACKIE, 38

• • •

Dating is exhausting! It's so tiring to have to chitchat and
cleverly reinvent yourself all the time. —MOLLY, 34

Not only do biology, time frames, and societal messages influence a woman's readiness to get engaged, exhaustion can also play a role. That's right, exhaustion from all of the energy expended that goes into the search for The One. Not to mention all the lip gloss!

Wondering what to make of all of this? Keep in mind that women and men can feel ready for marriage at different times. For women in their late twenties, thirties, or forties, it seems like they tend to get the "engagement itch" in just over a year of dating Mr. Right. Pre-engagement limbo comes in because not all (and I stress *not all*) but most guys are usually not ready at this point. More often they're not as speedy when it comes to knot tying.

I know it takes discipline not to track all the couples planning their big day sooner than yours, but every relationship grows at its own pace. The pace of your relationship should only matter when you truly feel ready to get married—and not because you feel you're supposed to be married. Pay less attention to the abrasive family member who nosily asks why you're not engaged yet and pay more attention to what it is you really want. A healthy, loving relationship isn't determined by how quickly he proposes. Let the diamond ring commercials entertain you—not influence you. You should be the one to determine when you feel enough is enough.

WHAT YOU SAID

In a survey asking 116 people what types of marriage pressure women deal with (respondents could check more than one, and most did), the top three that people checked were:

86 percent: biological (you can hear the clock ticking)
81 percent: from friends and family (who keep asking about the big day)
75 percent: societal (the hundreds of not-so-subtle bridal magazines do the job)

Also included:

39 percent: another summer booked with everyone else's weddings
3 percent: no pressure

Comments from those who checked "Other":

Pressure from myself to not be alone as I grow older—and
also because I want someone to share life with. —ELENA, 40

• • •

To be able to plan my future! —DINA, 34

• • •

Wanting a commitment so I know the relationship is stable.
—ANNIE, 26

• • •

[Women] are conditioned since birth to look forward
to the big day. —MIKE, 37

• • •

Patience helps [while in limbo] to some extent, but don't let
it get to the point where you feel like you're giving something
up in your life. Don't miss an opportunity because you're
busy waiting around for this guy. —EMILY, 31

• • •

I was always dealing with pressure. I'm the oldest sibling and
cousin and was the last to get married. —TANYA, 37

SHOW AND TELL

I asked women what influenced them to want to get engaged
when they did. This is what they said, along with a few of my own
thoughts, of course.

THE BLING
It wasn't a question of will he propose, it was a question of
what is he waiting for. I was pushing the timing, not the issue

of whether or not we'd end up together. He wanted us to be
dating longer. This only made me want the proposal more.
For the year before we got engaged, I was so obsessed that
it was the only thing I could think about. To be completely
honest, I wanted a ring! I don't think I cared so much about
the wedding as I did the ring. My Christmas list included
a night out at my favorite restaurant, theater tickets, and a
three-carat princess cut. I couldn't have been clearer.
I saw it as a status symbol. Not a material one, but as a
validation that I was part of a couple. I felt proud to be
part of a couple, and the ring was a way to have that all the
time. Another part of me wanted to have a
wedding before I was too old to wear
a big white gown! —TRACEY, 35

Women consider an engagement ring a symbol of connection, togetherness, and sometimes even social status. Knowing this, most
men spend a lot of time looking for the perfect ring that's special
and sentimental. And when they find out how much one costs,
they can't help but ponder, "Wow—why wouldn't we use that
money to travel around the world?"

So if he's not as enthusiastic as you are when you're looking at
the bling, don't be disappointed. Be aware of each other's differences here. We'll never hear, "Diamonds are a man's best friend."
His best bud is fluffier and not as sparkly as ours.

Tracey also addresses a great point. I hear women say they don't
want to miss out on wearing a poofy dress and everything that goes
along with that. They think they'd feel ridiculous for wanting
bridesmaids after a certain age. However, you can always go bridal
(or not). If you don't want to have two hundred guests at your wed-

ding when you're twenty-five—then don't. If you want all the hype when you're seventy—then go for it. Isn't it the bride's day, after all?

> The ring to a guy is just a really big expense.
> —STEPHANIE, 28

PLANNING THE BIG DAY SINCE YOU WERE FIVE

Ben and I had been together for just over a year when I started thinking about marrying him. Actually, come to think of it, he started it! He would ask me what kind of wedding I wanted; what kind of ring I wanted; who I would ask to be in my wedding party. These questions got my wheels turning! I'm a girl who has been planning her wedding since she was five. I would buy *Bride* magazine long before there was ever the prospect of a groom!

The whole topic of marriage came about in early August. I figured if he proposed around that time, I would have the requisite year to adequately plan. I knew that I loved Ben, that I wanted to be with him forever, and that he wanted the same. Once I knew that, I figured, why wait? It's like that line from *When Harry Met Sally,* "When you finally find the person you want to spend the rest of your life with, you want the rest of your life to start right now."

It was also the principle. We had been together for the standard amount of time, at least one year. Deep down I was nervous that if I didn't light a fire under his butt, he might be inclined to take his time, and then not only would I not have my wedding when I wanted it, but my friends and family might start asking questions, like "Is he really the one?" or "Do you think he's stalling for a reason?" That would be the

worst. It took five months of prodding and pressuring for
Ben to pop the question, and every day of those five months
was worse than the day before. It felt like it might as well
have been three lifetimes! The first year practically flew. It
was the last five months that felt like an eternity. It was like a
growing, insatiable sense of urgency for him to propose. The
longer he waited, the more I wanted it and the more
insistent I became. I couldn't sleep or eat or focus on
anything else. If he had taken any longer to ask . . . who
knows if I would have made it? —PAULA, 28

If you've been planning your wedding since you were five, it
makes sense that you would get excited once you've found the
groom. The final piece of the puzzle. But herein lies the rub. That
groom hasn't been planning his wedding since he was five. In fact,
he hasn't been planning anything for that long, except maybe how
to score season tickets.

If your wheels are spinning faster than your legs can keep up—
get grounded. As far as the "standard amount of time" for dating,
women and men have different criteria. To deal with your different schedules, first acknowledge that women are usually ready to
get married before men. This doesn't mean that a woman should
adjust to her boyfriend's schedule. Absolutely not. But understanding each other's different time zones helps lift some of the
pressure. Together you should come up with a time frame that is
comfortable for you both.

A TO-DO LIST

We had been together for nine months when I knew I
wanted to marry him. Once we hit the one-year mark, I was
anxious about getting engaged. I wanted to get married by

thirty. I already had a career, I had my MBA, and I wanted to have kids before it was too late. I constantly asked him about when we would get engaged. I couldn't help myself—I just kept bringing it up. This inevitably made him put it off more. We had already been living together and we were basically married, so I thought, "Why not just get married?"

I learned from him that guys think the opposite.

They think, "If you're already living together and sharing everything, then why get married?"

He ended up proposing after we had been together for eighteen months. This was a long time for me to hold out because it was stuck in my mind that in your late twenties, people date for a year and then get engaged. I know this is based on an idealistic timetable, but this was the template for me. Since I was a teenager I always thought you got married in your twenties and had kids by thirty. That was the vision I had in my head. I realize now I got this picture from television and society. —LISA, 33

Influences start early. From the time you picked up your first Barbie to picking out your first prom date, you were also picking up subtle messages about marriage, relationships, and time frames. I'll never forget—when I was twenty-six, my friend's younger sister asked, "When are you getting married?" She continued with "By the time I'm twenty-six, I'll be married with two kids." We have all done it—pictured years in advance where we'd be in life at a certain age. Always make room for adjustments. Getting to know yourself before getting married takes priority over any schedule. Sure, some women see marriage as the beginning of life together. However, many men express that they see marriage as an end to freedom and to youthfulness. Most of all, they see it as a time to kiss certain fantasies good-bye. And for a guy, that's hard to let go of. If you can't imagine what could possibly take so long—understand that he may be taking time to get ready himself.

HIS AND HERS

I was young when I knew this was the person that I wanted to marry. I became obsessed with getting engaged three years after dating. Basically, I wanted to know that my feelings were the same as his. When he would say that he loved me, it wasn't enough. I wanted a commitment with an engagement ring.
There were so many things that would make me want it more. It could be a celebrity wedding, a wedding scene in a movie, some diamond ring commercial. Flipping through television channels was no longer relaxing. I didn't even have friends who were married, but the media played such a part in showing how people fall in love.
They meet, fall in love, he proposes, she says yes. I didn't think about what getting married actually meant. But it turned out that was all that was on his mind. When my boyfriend and I talked about why he didn't feel ready to get engaged, he gave reasons that blew me away. He thought once he was married he could no longer have late-night pizza. He talked about needing enough money in the bank for a down payment on a house, having a certain income, and being more responsible.
He thought I would want kids right away, and he didn't feel ready for that. He was afraid that I wouldn't be a patient mother and was scared that we would argue in front of our children.

> He associated getting married with being a dad. This
> frustrated me, because I was talking about us getting
> engaged, and he would hear me talking about us
> being parents. —DIANA, 30

Just as women get messages from society about when they should get married, men get messages from society about what happens after they get married. They think about how they should be, what their life will be like, and what makes a good husband. Men have a picture in their minds as to what makes the ideal husband. Then they ask, "Am I that guy?" Sometimes these false images of the perfect hubby are actually leading men into a pressure-filled situation that women can easily misunderstand.

I once heard from a woman who said, "I'm so tired of my boyfriend making excuses that he's not ready to get engaged because he doesn't feel he makes enough money." Is this an excuse, or is this the real reason why he's putting on the brakes? Couples need to talk about their fears. Even though you may get wrapped up in the excitement of being a bride, it's important to talk to your soon-to-be fiancé about each other's values and visions for marriage—the house, the pitter-patters, the bank accounts. Preparing the best you can for the journey will help you with the takeoff.

Notes from the Professor, Dr. Judye Hess

There's pressure from society, but there is also a biological reality that women want to get the show on the road and get married so they can have kids before they're too old. There's a gender difference. Often guys are not looking for that. Guys are more often explorers and want to have different experiences with different women. The thought of tying the knot is more threatening for a guy. Whereas for some girls, by the time they're twelve, they're thinking about the kind of wedding dress they'll wear one day.

Women think their happiness is going to come from being married to the right person and having a family. Men aren't socialized that way. They're taught to believe that if they find the right career then they will be happy, and the wife and kid thing can happen later.

There's a different agenda and different priorities for men and women. A woman feels like a failure if she's not married and having kids, especially when her friends are. Whereas a guy feels like a failure when he doesn't have a job or doesn't know what career he's going into. Of course, somewhere down the road he too will feel like a failure if he's not in a relationship.

And sure, the media plays into it—there's the whole idea of Cinderella. The prince will take her away and save her.

First a woman has to play the waiting game to find the guy. Then she finds the guy and now there's this new waiting game she has to deal with. Of course it makes her frustrated and resentful.

A LITTLE WORKOUT SESSION

I heard from a woman who wanted a ring from her boyfriend who wasn't ready to give her one. They had only been dating for a year, and I asked, "What makes you feel ready to get engaged?" Her response: "Aside from love, I want the stability of marriage. I want to marry him because he's the right person for me and because I love him. Is there any other reason to want to get engaged?" Here's an exercise to help you figure that out:

1. Grab a piece of paper and a pen and at the top of the sheet, write: Why I want to get engaged right now at this point in my relationship.
2. Without editing, write down all of the reasons that come to mind for five straight minutes. And be honest. Put down even the embarrassing ones.
3. Once the five minutes are up, read through your list and circle the issues that feel most alive.
4. Take note of what each of these issues means to you. For example, if one of your reasons is "because all of my friends are already married," consider how it affects you and how it makes you feel and why.
5. Once you become aware of your influences and triggers, you can manage them. The first step is recognizing why they exist in the first place.

3

A Sweet Date Gone Sour: Expectation Downers

On our flight to Bermuda, my
boyfriend told me that I shouldn't
expect a proposal while we were
there. This only made me think he
was going to propose even more.

—TRACEY, 35

Spring. The season of engagement. I remember it well. The perfect yearlong plan for next year's spring wedding. The answering machine filling up with voices, bubbling over with excitement. "Hi, it's me! I have something to tell you! Call me back as soon as you can!" It's funny how our friends think these words disguise that these are actually "we just got engaged" phone calls.

My friends' boyfriends started handing out rings like candy—on birthdays, Valentine's Day, during vacations, over crème brûleé at fancy restaurants or hot dogs at the ballpark. Naturally, I imagined the impending when, where, and how my beau would give me my ring. My committee of women all seemed to agree that the time was soon, given that around a holiday or a mention of our upcoming weekend getaways they would respond with "You know it's going to happen!"

My boyfriend and I had already been living together for a while at this point, and there was no question that each of us was the other's The One. We covered the gamut as to how we imagined our lives together as husband and wife. We even discussed our very different visions for our wedding. My excitement for the details on our engagement started to intensify. (Perhaps that fateful day when he pulled me into a jewelry store to get my ring size had something to do with it.)

I noticed that whenever we would go away for a weekend, celebrate a holiday, or do anything out of the ordinary, I began to expect the proposal. Here, there, and everywhere. My symptoms from having these expectations began to worsen. Soon I found myself so absorbed with how an engagement would play out that I struggled to enjoy being in the moment of otherwise happy occasions. The perfect example: our trip to Hawaii.

It started when I shared the news with friends that we were taking off to the Big Island in a few weeks. Before I even packed a bag, we all gushed about how sweet he was to plan this trip. Finally he was going to get down on one knee! My girlfriends all would have bet their Jimmy Choos on it. One friend asked, "How do you think he'll propose?" We imagined when, where, and how he would pop the question in the honeymoon capital of the world.

It turns out that there was no proposal in Hawaii. I finally accepted it wasn't meant to be while we were in the checkout line at the hotel. After a long trip home, my drama continued when I walked into the house to a ringing telephone. I answered to voices on the other end shouting, "You got engaged, didn't you?!?"

As the months and years went on after this trip, I continued to expect the engagement during the most outrageous times, before finally exhausting myself of all hope. My most farfetched expectation (or should I say hallucination) was when he surprised me with tickets to see my favorite band, the Barenaked Ladies. The whole car ride down to Shoreline Amphitheatre, my heart was beating a little faster than usual. Somehow I got it into my head that he had coordinated with the concert venue to have the lead singer call out my name into a microphone between sets and shout, "Your beau wants to know if you'll marry him! What do you say?" My answer would flash in giant-size neon-bright letters on the backdrop screen of the stage. What a great story to share with the grandkids.

Several songs went by, and still no special announcement for me. I waited patiently. Would it happen during the next song . . . or two . . . or three . . . ? As you probably guessed, there was no proposal at Shoreline. Reality eventually set in after the show ended. I remember standing there dumbstruck, watching the stage crew clear away the instruments. I don't think my sixth-grade teacher, Mrs. Simpson, would applaud my creative imagination at a time like this.

I was obsessed. If we were at a romantic restaurant, I would think the ring was hidden somewhere in my dessert. When he handed me a bouquet of long-stemmed roses, I inspected them, convinced the ring was attached to the bunch. Each time I came to the realization that the ring wasn't in my dessert, tied to a rose, or at the Barenaked Ladies concert, my face would flush and my stomach would sink a little more from the disappointment.

What was happening to me? Couldn't I appreciate a good evening unless it ended in a proposal? I wanted to hide in my shame for becoming compulsively ring hungry.

The tension in our relationship started to get worse. It was so long ago since we'd gotten my ring size, I was sure it would change by the time he got around to buying anything. I kept telling myself to get a grip, but time was getting the best of me. As each opportunity for him to pop the question slipped by, like my birthday, New Year's Eve, and Valentine's Day, my resentment built.

THE EXPECTATION DOWNER

When we truly expect that he's finally going to pop the question and then doesn't, we're crushed. No matter how fabulous an event is, not getting the ring when we thought we would can easily squash everything wonderful into a pancake of disappointment.

Looking back, I see how much I could have enjoyed but didn't because I was too distracted wondering if there was a ring in his pocket. Instead of being in the moment on a birthday, on a special holiday, or while away someplace romantic for a weekend (or pathetically enough, even at a rock concert), my mind was elsewhere. I wasn't appreciating what was right in front of me. I regret missing out on all the times I could have enjoyed if only I didn't let my expectations get ahead of me.

A friend recently shared how excited she was about her upcoming vacation with her boyfriend to Key West. Not only was she eager for the warm weather, the poolside daiquiris, and a fabulous spa treatment, she was eager for her beau to get down on one knee. Her voice screamed with anticipation. "I think he's going to propose!" Wait a minute. I had heard this song before. My reaction was "Uh-oh."

I felt a tropical storm coming on. I wanted to jump through the phone, hug her and plead, "Please just enjoy yourself. You've been looking forward to this vacation for so long. Don't let another round of 'he proposes, he proposes not' ruin your trip."

Since my phone-jumping skills are rusty, we just chatted. I focused her energy on the sure bets of her vacation. It was safe to expect a sunny forecast, drinks with umbrellas, time to relax, and even a sea salt scrub at the spa. What wasn't written on the itinerary was whether or not her man might be feeling especially flexible at the knee that week.

We also decided to lay out the options on how she could protect herself from an "expectation downer." Option A: She could express that she's extremely excited about this next phase of their relationship and she'd appreciate knowing beforehand if she should be getting her nails done for any particular reason. Maybe a little extra attention her hand would be getting soon?

Issue not yet solved, as she had a problem with Option A. She wanted the proposal to be a surprise, just like They say it's supposed to be. You know . . . They. De Beers. Danielle Steel. Hallmark. Them.

If she brought up any getting-engaged lingo, it could ruin his plans. And who knows? He might even add more time to the proposal. She didn't want to risk the chance that he might drag out the waiting period.

Okay, on to Option B: She could be aware of her expectations and choose to manage them. She could try on the attitude "If it happens, it happens. If it doesn't, it doesn't." Her initial response to this: "Yeah, right."

We joked and laughed about a possible (albeit ridiculous) Option C. The way to prevent the downer would be to chalk it up to how cliché it would be for him to propose at a romantic resort. Wouldn't it make more sense to obsess on regular workdays to avoid bringing down all the special occasions? She was dazzled by the comedy of this scenario, an Option C concocted to show the humor of it all.

So there it was. We landed safely on Option A meets Option B. She agreed that when and if expectations got the best of her, she would share her feelings with her boyfriend instead of holding them in. This would help her avoid building up the resentment and disappointment. Sometimes we have to work at managing our hopes, dreams, and expectations, so that they don't take over the special moments.

KEEPING IT SWEET

Society has done a magnificent job of getting women psyched up for the big day. After all, we keep hearing that this wedding is supposed to be the best event of our life. Naturally, there will be times when our heart races a little faster as we think, "This is it! He's going to propose!" What a downer when by the end of the night our left hand is still bare.

A LITTLE WORKOUT SESSION

It's normal to have expectations, just as it's normal to experience disappointment. And there's a way to prepare:

1. Acknowledge your mindset and that you're expecting something big to happen.
2. Since you've probably imagined what would happen if your expectation played out, also imagine what it would be like if it didn't.
3. Think about how you want to be if things don't go as you had hoped. What would your behavior be like? How would you respond?
4. Remember, you don't have to let the downer take over—you can take over the downer.

Even with all the effort put into staying in the here and now, it's still tough to manage the feelings left from an expectation downer. Many of us have been there. We also know how a little more attitude develops after each disappointment. That's right, watch out! We can't help but think we're living alone with humiliation, since every woman we see has a left hand that sparkles. We wonder why it's so hard for us, when it looks so easy for everyone else. But is it really that easy for everyone else?

The multibillion-dollar wedding industry shows us engagement proposals that seem like a fairy tale. However, getting engaged is not a fairy tale. It's as real as it gets (other than the actual "I do"). It's a relationship transition, and transition can be difficult. I don't know about you, but for as long as I can remember I've been hearing about how men don't like change. Proposals don't always happen the way they do in the movies (disappointing, I know). But in actuality, this isn't necessarily a bad thing. It's the open and honest conversations about our fears and hopes that allow us to grow. So why not keep it real?

If you want to avoid an expectation downer, couples can decide together when, where, and how they will get engaged. Celebrate taking the relationship to the next level. And remember, a woman could always propose instead of waiting it out and having the limbo drive her crazy (more on that in chapter 9).

Getting engaged isn't just up to him, it's about the couple. I understand guys are sensitive about their roles here, and they don't want to be written out of the script. I hear all the time from women, "My boyfriend gets upset when I bring up getting engaged. He says it's up to him to propose." We know they move slower toward marriage. But if a guy has been given plenty of time to make his move and he chooses to do nothing, then he should expect that his role is going to be recast. Or worse, he may be booted out of the show altogether.

At the same time, I understand that many women still want the man to take the reins on this one. Whether she's a career-driven woman from the city or someone who has chosen to pursue the arts in a small town, most women tell me they want their beau to be the one to propose. So here we are, dealing with expectation downer after expectation downer.

Consider New Year's Eve. There's always so much hype around this night. So much pressure to have the Best Time Ever. It's as if your entire next year's happiness is dependent upon that one count-down. You even have to find someone special to kiss when the clock tells you it's time to pucker up. New Year's Eve is supposed to be the highlight evening of the year. But every year, without fail, I was dis-appointed. It never measured up to my expectations. It wasn't until I let go of the expectations that I started to have fun again. I enjoyed the evening for what it was, one simple evening dressed up with confetti and champagne. Doesn't it ring true that when you don't ex-pect anything at all, then that's when you have the time of your life?

Ultimately, the best way to survive expectation downers is to understand your man. Guys don't have engagement radar. A woman I know shared her story with me. She was taking a roman-tic sunset walk along the beach with her beau in Maui thinking, "What an amazing place for him to propose." She was sure he was thinking the same—and then taken aback by his response when she asked, "Honey, what are ya thinking about?" His words: "I'm wondering if the Yankees made it into the playoffs. I'll just check the score of tonight's game when we get back to the hotel." Women can pick out a number of different scenarios all at once as to when it coulda/shoulda/woulda been a great time for a pro-posal. Men focus on one thing at a time.

FAQ

Question: I'm going away with my boyfriend next month, and I can't stop thinking that he'll propose. My birthday was a disaster because there wasn't a proposal. I don't want this vacation to be ruined too. Any tips on managing things?

Answer: Perhaps the actual issue isn't whether or not he'll propose on your upcoming vacation. Maybe it's that you're tired of waiting for the proposal and the vacation itself is a trigger. You could play "mind over matter" and think of the vacation for what it is and not as a proposal destination. It's a chance for you to spend alone time with the man you love. Or you can have a conversation with your boyfriend. Tell him how you're excited about your upcoming trip but at the same time you're feeling a little anxious thinking about a potential proposal. Why not check in with each other to see if you're on the same page as to when an engagement may be happening?

MORE SHOW AND TELL

Not that misery loves company—but let's face it, she kinda does. Healing begins when we realize another person can fully relate to what we are experiencing. I bring to you these Sweet Dates Gone Sour:

THE DOWN-ON-ONE-KNEE FAKE-OUT

It was Valentine's Day. My boyfriend called and said, "I'm taking you out and I'm not telling you what I'm doing."

He picks me up at work. As I walk out toward his car, I see
him kneeling down next to the passenger's door with a long-
stemmed rose between his teeth. I was freaking out. I looked
like a deer in headlights [thinking he was going to propose].
He says, "This is a clue to what's going to happen later." We
go to his house, he cooks me dinner—the whole thing.
Suddenly he says, "We've got to get going. We have an event
to go to." He drives us downtown. We walk out of the
parking garage and right in front of us is Tiffany's. I was
thinking, "Is he bringing me to Tiffany's to get a ring?" I was
playing it out in my mind. I think he's taking me to Tiffany's
and I get to pick out any ring I want. At the same time I'm
ready to kill him because he shouldn't actually buy the ring
from Tiffany's. Anyway, we never went to Tiffany's. Turns out,
he took me to some tango show. And in the show the
dancers were down on one knee with a rose in their mouth.
And then it all made sense. I don't think he had a clue. We
haven't talked about it to this day. —CARLEY, 28

When a ringless Valentine's Day comes and goes, every special occasion becomes the No. 1 time of year to expect a proposal. (After
all, isn't President's Day romantic?) If you notice that waiting is
getting in the way of your happiness, why continue to wait? Instead, decide together when and where the engagement will happen. Keep in mind that it's important to be able to communicate
with your partner. Throughout your life as husband and wife, there
will be topics that are difficult to talk about. It's important that you
can talk to each other. Getting engaged is about both of you. If you
would rather your boyfriend pop the question the traditional way,
then give him the chance to propose on his own. Once you make
that choice, don't let your enthusiasm get ahead of you.

THE JEWELRY BOX MIXUP

It was my birthday, we had been together for five years, and I
figured we'd get engaged soon. I guess you could say I
started waiting for the ring. I didn't think he would propose
on my birthday—that would be too ordinary. [That night] we
were going out for dinner, and when I finished getting ready I
went downstairs to wait for him. He walked into the den, sat
next to me on the couch, and handed me a jewelry box. I
started shaking! I assumed my diamond was in there. I
opened the box, and instead of a ring, it was a beautiful
watch. It was gorgeous, but I was completely blown away and
perplexed because in the back of my mind I didn't
understand why he didn't just give me the ring.
We get to the restaurant, and I have a little panic
attack. I felt like I was in my own little hell trying to
figure out what was going on. I should have been having
a great time—we were at my favorite restaurant,
I just got a beautiful gift—but I felt like he threw me
a huge curveball. I couldn't stop thinking about
why he didn't just put the money for
a watch toward a ring.
Christmas came soon after, and I was sure he was going to
propose. He gave me this huge box to unwrap. I was so
excited thinking this was one of those box-inside-of-a-box
sort of treats. I ripped off the bows and all the wrapping
paper . . . and it's a cappuccino maker. I did mention once
in passing I wanted one, so I figured he's trying to catch
me off guard. So I start looking around in this big box
to see where the ring could be. But it was really just
a cappuccino maker.

—MYA, 32

If the expectation downer gets you when you don't expect it—don't be hard on yourself, and roll with your emotions. Be in the moment. You can (a) excuse yourself to phone a friend who will understand or (b) you can talk about what you're feeling with your boyfriend. You're in this together, and it's okay to share with him how you feel. You don't have to sit through dinner, trying to keep your panic down.

I'm going to take this opportunity to provide a tip to the guys who might be reading this. We appreciate your kind intentions, truly. But the universal rule is, if your girlfriend is expecting a proposal, never ever give her a gift that comes in a box that even slightly resembles one for an engagement ring. Just thought I'd save you the headache.

THE VACATION EXPECTATION

Italy—the perfect place to get engaged. It was one
of the most anticipated trips Glen and I had ever taken.
In our seven years of dating, this was our first
romantic vacation together.
I was expecting a proposal. As soon as we finalized
our plans, I thought about it all the time and was trying
so hard not to bring it up or ask anything about it before
we left. Once our plane landed, I felt as though my
heart would burst, I was so happy.
A few days passed, and I started to wonder when he
was going to ask and what he was planning. One night
while we were out, I started to feel down. I began to see that
maybe a proposal was all in my head. I had a few more glasses
of wine and told him, "I just want to celebrate, since
we're on vacation, sweetie!"
That celebration turned out to be a forty-minute buzz
that quickly faded into anger and negativity. Once we got

back to our hotel, he could tell something was wrong. We sat
out on the balcony, and the tears just rolled down my
cheeks. He kept asking what was wrong, and I was so
humiliated that all I wanted was to go home.
Finally, I looked at him dead-on and asked, "You weren't
planning anything special during this trip, were you?"
He looked at me blankly. It looked like I hurt him. He asked,
"Uh, what do you mean?"
I let it all out. I cried and cried and asked myself and
him, "Why am I so ready for this? When is it going to happen?"
He listened the way a best girlfriend would. He comforted
me and told me he could really see how I felt. It was painful,
but I needed him to let me be sad. We ended up talking
through it. The next day I woke up and felt peaceful.
It wasn't because a proposal was on the way. Instead, I realized
I had my best friend at my side.
Our trip had a few days left in it, and we finally started to
enjoy ourselves and each other. We came home with a
special feeling that we could work through things together.
Four months later he asked my parents' permission for my
hand in marriage. Right now we're planning the details
of our fall wedding! —SONYA, 30

The way Glen listened to Sonya shows that sometimes we just
need to let out how we feel in order to take the weight off our
shoulders. This also goes for guys stuck in limbo. As Sonya was
able to talk about her disappointment, sometimes guys just need
to voice their fears.

Notes from the Professor, Dr. Judye Hess

I don't know if this would take away the mystery or the spontaneity, but a woman could share her feelings. Because now they've gone away on a trip, and she's wondering if he's going to propose. At the same time, he just planned this romantic getaway, and he thinks she's going to be thrilled.

If they talk about everything else, why can't they talk about this? She could say, "I wish this weren't the case, but I'm getting all excited about the prospect that we're going to get engaged on this trip, and it's really getting the better of me."

A LITTLE WORKOUT SESSION

When you and your boyfriend arrive at that vacation spot or have a night planned out on the town and you find yourself distracted from enjoying what is in front of you right now ("Would he give me a princess cut or a round solitaire?"), remind yourself to stay present. It's presence that enables us not to miss out on what is actually happening in a moment.

1. Get centered.
2. Take in your surroundings. Acknowledge the beauty of where you are, what's around you, and who you are with.
3. Pay attention and focus in on what it is you two are sharing right now, without thinking ahead to any proposal.
4. If you're having trouble getting centered, take some time for yourself and write out your feelings to get them out of your system.
5. If negative feelings are building ("What, no ring?!"), remember you don't have to go through this passage alone. You can share your feelings with your beau—without blaming.

4

His Cool Feet: I'm Not Ready

I got a voice mail message on my
cell the other day from a friend
of mine. He sounded like he was
at a funeral. Which probably
means he just got engaged.

—DAVE, 38

ere's the big question we all want answered. It's been
asked by many and avoided by many more. Why does it
take men so long to pop the question?

I wouldn't be writing this book if I was shy about asking,
"Dude, what's the deal with dragging your feet?" I'm not scared to
bug a hesitant man: "What do you mean you want to get married,
but you're just not ready?" And believe me, what I've found out
certainly makes for a very beefy chapter.

For starters, let's look at it this way. Think about the different
scenes that play out for women and men when they each announce their engagement. It's like watching two different movies:
a happy chick flick versus a painful drama.

Cinema #1's love story begins. Action! As soon as a ring is
placed on a woman's finger and the long-awaited words "Will you
marry me?" are asked, utter giddiness and elation fill the air. Her
mind begins spinning . . . "Summer or spring wedding?" "Roses or
tulips?" "Black tie or casual chic?" Before he's closed the box and

gotten up off of his knee, she's silently writing out the guest list and counting out her bridesmaids. For years she may have been planning for the big day, but now it's official. Making decisions about chocolate-covered strawberries is finally a sweet chocolate-covered reality.

Cut to the next scene. The bride-to-be excitedly reaches for her cell phone, and one by one she speed-dials those on her A-list. If one BFF can't be reached, our heroine simply leaves one of those candid not-so-mysterious messages. Her coy voice says, "Hey, there's something I have to tell you. (*Giggle*) Call me back when you can."

Although her friends automatically know what the "something" means (not exactly secret code), they don't dare spoil the occasion. They act surprised when they return her call. They gush with enthusiasm. "Congratulations!" "Were you surprised?" "How'd he propose?"

Cast in a supporting role for this scene is a woman who's waiting for her own ring. She's happy for her friend, but at the same time can't help wondering why her man hasn't popped the question. It's only human nature for her to obsess over how the newly engaged has been dating for exactly three months, four days, and two hours less than she and her boyfriend (but who's counting?). Anyway, she quickly snaps herself out of the what-about-me mode and briefly meditates on the mantra "Do not compare. Do not compare."

As girlfriends share the big news, they chat away on their cell phones in their most cheerful voices. Sometimes only dogs can hear the high-pitched squeals of joy during this phone celebration. They relive detail after detail of the proposal. "Tell me, tell me, tell me!" Given the nitty-gritty tell-all nature of the conversation about such a long-awaited moment, it couldn't possibly end with "Okay, see ya later," could it? No, no, no. After the hangup comes the plan to get together for the mini-celebration—either lunch at the local café, martinis after work, or appointments for mani-and-pedis. This is when they go over everything. Every detail. Again. But this time, a new guest star has the spotlight. The diamond ring.

The friends get together and give the bride-to-be warm hugs filled with gusto they didn't even know they had. They check out the ring. They try it on. Some will even place their hand on an imaginary steering wheel to get the feel of what it would be like to have a sparkler while driving. (Don't we all do that?)

The mini-celebration exists so the newly engaged can relive the story of her engagement (just one, two, or twelve more times). It's a chance for the bride-to-be to now address a different type of question: "Have you picked a date?" "What kind of dress?" "What did your parents say?"

So in this romantic theatrical storyboard, we've experienced the phone hysteria and the mini-celebration. Could there be more? Absolutely! There's a finishing touch—a mailbox once filled with other girls' wedding invites is now brimming with Hallmark cards. Friends sign, seal, and deliver their congrats, and there's always at least a heart or two doodled somewhere on the envelope. And that's a wrap. A total blockbuster! Two ring fingers up!

Playing next door in Cinema #2 is another movie—more like a short film—on a guy announcing his engagement. Our hero certainly isn't silently counting out how many groomsmen, daydreaming about flower petals, or giggling with his elated buddies over a cocktail. He puts in a few short phone calls (his folks, brother, best buddy), then it's business as usual. The thought of registering at the Home Depot for the newest DeWALT may cross his mind, but it's more likely he's pondering his bachelor party. And that's it. The popcorn didn't even get cold.

It's no wonder announcing an engagement is like two different scenes for women and men. Just look at our choices of movies and their heroes and heroines. Women want TiVo to pick up the happily-ever-after romance, while guys want it to record James Bond movies. Bond is surrounded by women in skimpy bikinis. He's out kicking butt. He's not tied down. No one tells Bond to take out the garbage.

The hit movie *Sideways* paints a pretty realistic picture. There's the fabulous scene when Miles introduces Jack to the bartender at his favorite restaurant and shares the news about Jack getting married next weekend. In response to an introduction involving wedding bells, the bartender says, "My condolences, man." And there it is! No congratulations. No excited exclamations. Just the agony of defeat and a shocking ending full of shared suffering and pain.

What else do guys get when they share their news of a recent engagement? There's "When's the funeral?" or "Good luck, man." Ah, there's also the old hand-to-shoulder embrace accompanied by a look of caution and a shaking head—which could mean absolutely anything.

I was at a wedding where the father of the bride's toast included "And when the kids told us they were getting married, I looked at Dan and said, 'Do you know what you're getting yourself into?'" All two hundred guests laughed. The couple took it well.

Many men think of getting married as an end. How can they not, with all of this fanfare? Their friends talk about it in terms of "Well, this is it." But some men go so far as to describe getting married as a sort of death. They're saying good-bye to a part of who they are. Good-bye to the side of them that likes being a bachelor, likes their freedom and their independence.

My fiancé and I were driving up to the church to meet with
the priest a few months before our wedding. The church
happened to be down the street from the hospital where my
fiancé was born. He joked, as he pointed from one place to
the other, "This is where I was born . . . and this
is where I die." —RANDI, 34

At the announcement of an engagement, while women are
jumping up and down with each other giggling, "Let me see the
ring," men are extending good-luck wishes and condolences. Guys
don't send Hallmarks. They send Get Out of Jail Free cards they
swiped from their old Monopoly boards, humorous pokes that
might help their doomed friend.

So what's causing all this doom and gloom? Why is he dragging
his feet?

A STUDY ON THE MATTER

In 2002, Barbara Dafoe Whitehead and David Popenoe led a study,
"Why Men Won't Commit: Exploring Young Men's Attitudes About
Sex, Dating, and Marriage." Their research was for the National
Marriage Project's annual report, *The State of Our Unions: The
Social Health of Marriage in America, 2002.* They conducted eight
focus groups of sixty unmarried men between the ages of twenty-
five and thirty-three, throughout northern New Jersey, Chicago,
Washington D.C., and Houston.

Here are Whitehead and Popenoe's top ten reasons why men
are slow to commit:

1. They can get sex without marriage more easily than in
   times past.

2. They can enjoy the benefits of having a wife by cohab-iting rather than marrying.
3. They want to avoid divorce and its financial risks.
4. They want to wait until they are older to have chil-dren.
5. They fear that marriage will require too many changes and compromises.
6. They are waiting for the perfect soul mate, and she hasn't yet appeared.
7. They face few social pressures to marry.
8. They are reluctant to marry a woman who already has children.
9. They want to own a house before they get a wife.
10. They want to enjoy single life as long as they can.

When I was going through my own pre-engagement limbo, I started by drilling my friends' husbands for a man's point of view. And when I started writing *His Cold Feet,* I spread the word that I was looking to hear from men who didn't feel ready to propose at the time their girlfriends were expecting them to. Eventually word got around, and here are some of the common issues that kept coming up:

- What-ifs/fear of the unknown
- What are they giving up vs. what are they getting
- Will sex become infrequent
- Is there a Bigger Better Deal out there
- Will they lose their freedom
- Will they have to grow up
- Will they be trapped
- What is expected of them

We know where he's not coming from—the jeweler's. But let's take a careful look at each of these stressful pressures that men seem to run into. Then we can begin to understand where he *is* coming from.

THE WHAT-IFS

Committing to be with one person for the rest of my life was very scary. I was afraid that I would wake up unhappy in five years and regret it. —ANDY, 32

This is a big one. With the thought of marriage, guys talk about having spiraling thoughts of what-ifs. They can show up whether a guy is thinking about kissing his single days good-bye ("What if I miss out on something?") or when he's imagining turning into his parents ("What if we get divorced?"). Once the imagination gets going, there's no end. On and on and on . . .

What-ifs can easily freak anyone out of doing practically anything. We've all been there. Even something as simple as shoe shopping for a vacation can become an indecisive mess. "These cute sandals fit well in the store, but what if after walking around a bit, they end up rubbing and I get a blister? Then my vacation will be ruined. Maybe I shouldn't buy them." It's all about fear of the unknown. Jumping into something without knowing the outcome is scary—scary enough that it can make a guy want to buy more time . . . and more time . . . and even more time.

When I was thinking of moving to California from Boston, it was a what-if nightmare. I wanted to go, but then I'd start up with "What if I don't like it?" My dad would say, "Well, if you don't like it you can always move back." Sounded so simple. I even had plenty of frequent flyer miles racked up, but still I couldn't see it this way. I felt like once I headed west, that was it—I'd be stuck forever. My college friend Lor made her own jump before I went out to Cali. It wasn't much different from standing on the edge of a pool and saying to a willing fellow swimmer, "You see if it's cold first." I watched how she survived the leap from New York City to San Francisco. About a year later I joined her in our new city.

Just like moving, getting married takes some getting used to. There's an adjustment period. There are times when it's not so easy. But all anyone can ever do is give it a try, a really good try, and be accepting of the ups and downs. And know that if worst comes to worst, there are options on how to get to a better place.

Since marriage is such a huge decision, it's important to give it careful thought. And because it's so important, a mix of emotions are bound to surface. To help deal with the jitters, it's important to recognize whether it's good old-fashioned fear whispering in your ear or there's something in the relationship that's an actual cause for concern.

Use the following exercise to help identify which one your boyfriend is dealing with. It might even help you with your own fears, since men aren't the only ones tackling this great unknown. Once you do get engaged, you might notice that you yourself are starting to get a little nervous too. That's perfectly normal. Engagement is a big step. One that leads to bigger things. Marriage. Commitment. A lifetime. Not light and fluffy concepts. So both of you need some time to clarify what it is about marriage itself that might be knotting up everyone's stomach. Ask these questions of yourself and your beau:

- Does my fear of getting married have to do with issues outside of the relationship? (What if it doesn't work, what if we don't get along in ten years, etc.)

- Or does my fear of getting married have to do with issues about my partner and the relationship? (We don't seem to have the same values, we don't seem to relate to one another, etc.)

If you have spinning thoughts of "What if we fall out of love?" or "What if we get a divorce?" you can relax. These are all common concerns regarding marriage, fear of the unknown, and the scariness that appears when there are no guarantees.

On the other hand, fears (rational or not) might be signs that the relationship isn't as healthy as it should be. When this is the case, certain things need to be addressed—what's acceptable, what can be changed, and what's a deal breaker. If fears are tied in with concerns about your partner and the relationship, clarify and consider the value of these concerns. How heavily do they weigh on each of you as a future spouse? We each have our own values and thresholds for what gets on our nerves. While dirty socks on the bathroom floor and being late once in a while may push your buttons, they obviously carry a different weight than "red flags"— such as if you often feel hurt by your partner or if you have different ideals or basic principles. You can both take time to identify what's causing any hesitancy. Fix your eyes forward! Ears open! Be willing to talk and work things through.

When you get to know where the fears stem from, it'll help you get in touch with whether either of you is afraid of marriage itself or is reluctant to put a forever time frame on your specific relationship. If it's a strong partnership, teammates should be able to huddle up and talk about what keeps them from wanting to cross that finish line. Collaborating together about fears, expectations, and hopes can lead to a check in the win column.

We constantly hear references about how men don't like

change. (Why else do they hold on to sneakers way past their prime?) Without a crystal ball it's hard to know how any decision will play out. For those who have a tough time with change and making decisions—the what-ifs can be difficult to hurdle.

Your guy may not want to list all of his what-ifs to you. But when you both talk about your fears, it helps to normalize them and put them into perspective. Share with him some of your own what-ifs. When we openly talk about weddings as such joyous occasions, it gets confusing when other emotions, anxieties, and fears are added to the mix. While you might be wondering, "What's wrong with me? Why hasn't he proposed?" there's a chance he's wondering, "What's wrong with me? Why can't I just be happy and ask for her hand?"

THE COST

I was talking to Dan about what keeps a guy stuck on proposing. He was fresh out of business school, so it didn't surprise me when he gave his opinion in economic terms, saying, "It's all because of the opportunity cost." In my humble opinion, not marrying the person you love is "the opportunity lost."

Here's Dan's theory: Guys think about what this decision is going to cost them. Forget financial. You both have paid for enough movies, dinners, and holiday gifts (and we've also heard nightmare tales beyond those incidentals). Dan's talking in terms of intangible costs—freedom, single-hood, and independence, things without a price tag but with high value.

I think it's a phenomenon that all men address. Whether a guy jumps into marriage or drags his feet, reminders of the opportunity cost are everywhere. Opportunity cost management isn't over once he walks down the aisle. As we move from having friends who were mostly single or

newlyweds to friends who have five-plus years
of marriage under their belts, I think the implications
of choosing one path or another years earlier become
more real in men's minds. Like those ads that read NO
PAYMENTS 'TIL NEXT YEAR. Next year does come, and the
payments come due.

—DAN, 36

What is "opportunity cost"? I turned to Economics A–Z at Economist.com to find out.

> The true cost of something is what you give up to get it. This includes not only the money spent in buying (or doing) the something, but also the economic benefits (utility) that you did without because you bought (or did) that particular something and thus can no longer buy (or do) something else. For example, the opportunity cost of choosing to train as a lawyer is not merely the tuition fees, price of books, and so on, but also the fact that you're no longer able to spend your time holding down a salaried job or developing your skills as a footballer. These lost opportunities may represent a significant loss of utility. Going for a walk may appear to cost nothing, until you consider the opportunity forgone to use that time earning money. Everything you do has an opportunity cost. Economics is primarily about the efficient use of scarce resources, and the notion of opportunity cost plays a crucial part in ensuring that resources are indeed being used efficiently.

Is this why, after purchasing a ring, guys don't hand it over right away? Are they going over the implications of their decision again and again in their heads? Sometimes the rock is tucked away in a drawer for months. While women are thinking of the opportunity gain (togetherness, family, couple-hood), are guys thinking about the opportunity gone (independence, BBD, single-hood)?

For women it starts as early as age three when we pick a best friend, or the first time we play house. Although men also want a family and enjoy being part of a couple, they know these things will cost them some of their individuality. As basic as it sounds, it's similar to when they research buying a car: Men are programmed to evaluate and compare the value of one thing to another. They're evaluating the cost of their decision on getting married—what it will cost them. It's not that he doesn't have faith in you. It's more like how you watch him visit CNET.com to compare editorial reviews for one digital camera over another. He wants to make the most informed, best decision possible. He wants to be sure.

FROM SEX KITTEN TO HOUSE CAT

For some men, once they get married they think life is over. Guys think about how when they get married, they're only going to have sex with one person for the rest of their life. Men are very sexually oriented—thinking about being with one woman is difficult. Panic sets in. —PHIL, 54

The thought of being with one woman for the rest of his life—that can be unsettling for a guy. And there are also stories about how a couple's sex life cools down after tying the knot. While we're out buying hot new La Perla lingerie for the honeymoon, guys are getting an earful about how they should get used to granny panties and sudden "headaches." I'm not sure if guys laugh or cry when they hear the popular joke thrown around at wedding receptions:

"What food ends a woman's sex drive? Wedding cake." To them, this is no laughing matter.

In the same category of "What if she changes?" is "What if she stops taking care of herself?" I know this sounds superficial, and believe me, I don't love the idea of this either, but it's worth mentioning. The common misconception about women adding a few sizes once they add a Mrs. is enough to stop any married runway model in her catwalk tracks—why do men think these things?

Some men worry that getting married means a wife returns from the honeymoon and immediately trades in the silkies from Victoria's Secret for the frumpies from Target's sale rack. When women first start dating a man, we make that extra effort to pick up a little something to surprise him at bedtime. And what about all the rummaging through our roommate's closet for that perfect outfit to wear out on a Saturday night date—so sleek, trim, and sexy? Looking our best is a priority when we're trying to reel him in. Maybe you think he doesn't notice or appreciate it because he forgets to say, "You look beautiful." Well, let me tell you, they sure do notice once all that effort goes astray.

This doesn't mean dressing up in stilettos every night to keep him interested. I hate heels. I love my sweats. But I think my husband gets a little freaked out when two days go by and I'm still wearing the same hooded sweatshirt and lounge pants. And it certainly doesn't help clear a single guy's mind when he sees how some of his friends' wives have transformed from totally hot babe to totally letting-it-all-go wife.

The focus on the physical also relates to a guy's fear that a couple's sex life goes down the tubes once they get married. You've probably heard this joke too: "Did you hear about the new married couple? They have sex almost every night. Almost on Friday night, almost on Saturday night, almost on Sunday night." It certainly struck a nerve when I told it to a newly engaged guy friend of mine. His face turned as white as the 800-thread count on his and his fiancée's bed.

Thinking about the possibility of his sex life going downhill isn't the entire reason why a guy doesn't propose. But it's just a little something added on to his list of fears—a list that's getting so long it could wrap around his ankles, an obvious deterrent to running to the altar. Just knowing that this may cross his mind can help you understand a few of the fears. He isn't afraid of your sex life itself. It's just one of those things he's been hearing about for ages, an unwelcome rite of passage that all married men must go through—when they give up their single life, they give up their sex life. This probably contributes to him saying, "I like the way things are—why change anything?"

THE BBD

> For some guys their fear of getting married
> might be that they want to be able to play the field.
> But that will change. —RYAN, 34

The Bigger Better Deal. BBD. It's rather self-explanatory. It's guy talk for being on the lookout for something better than what they've got. This is another one we can easily get caught up in by always wondering where the grass is greener.

How do you define the BBD? He says:

> Illusion. —KENNY, 28

73

It's like the dog with the bone in the reflection.

—FRANK, 44

• • •

A wife without undesirable traits.

—MITCH, 25

She says:

The thought that a better, more interesting, more fun, or more attractive woman will come along after committing to someone. —AMANDA, 33

• • •

The bigger-boob, better-attitude, perfect woman who is out there waiting for him to meet her. All women know she doesn't exist. —BOBBI, 24

• • •

The mysterious perfect partner that has a chance of being a better match for you than the person you're about to make a commitment to. —CHARLOTTE, 27

Once you get stuck on this concept, it's tough to appreciate and enjoy what you have. It takes over and becomes a big distraction. So right before guys are about to take the leap, they come down with a bout of the BBD. Instead of focusing on what they've got, they focus on what they imagine they could have.

When I interviewed Amanda and Adam to get the scoop on their story, a story that began nine and a half years ago and ended with a ring, I asked Adam for his take on the Bigger Better Deal. He explained, "In the back of every guy's mind is this looming 'What if there's something better out there for me?'"

Amanda chimed in, "Women think that too. I just don't know what's the difference. Why is it a BBD for men?"

Adam shared: "Because women have fantasized about getting married and playing house since they were two, right? It's basically part of the story of your life. With guys, it's not part of their story. Part of their story is the conquest of making money and being a powerful or famous person. That's our story. And that has nothing to do with getting married. The mythology is totally different for the guy and the girl. James Bond is our guy. That's what we play when we're two. He's not married."

Amanda's rebuttal: "There are men who want to get married."

Adam said, "Yeah, but what, it's like five percent or something. You see the difference of how little girls play and how little boys play. I think it has to do with the difference of how we're socialized. There's a difference in how we think about the world."

When I checked in with my friend Dave about this, he explained, "If you ask men if they want to get married they'd say yes. They just don't want to get married right now. They want to live out the James Bond or Hugh Hefner fantasy first. Then they'll get married and have kids and do the family thing. There's a part of a guy that wants to get married. But then there's another part that doesn't want to settle for anything less than the fantasy."

So why have we always considered the BBD as strictly a guy focus, even though women are also culprits? Women compare their boyfriends, their relationships, to what's out there. "Josh proposed to Mary. What's wrong with my boyfriend?" "Liza's boyfriend always sends her flowers." "I wonder what my life would be like if I was still with my old beau Jimmy."

If women are out on the dating scene, it might just take a Date #3 before the new guy doesn't stand a chance. "He doesn't seem healthy. He ordered two sodas at dinner, and everything he ordered was fried." "Everything was going great, and then we went up to his place. His apartment was so messy!"

Then the difference hit me.

From conversations I've had about the whole Bigger Better Deal hoopla, this is how it seems to boil down: Men fantasize about what *could be* out there. Women compare what they have to what they *already know* is out there (old boyfriends, their friends' boyfriends). If there aren't any real contenders for comparison, the woman thinks she can change her guy into the BBD—or should I say train him into the BBD. Trading in his torn T's for collared polos. Getting him to see that when referring to his "nice" pants, she's not talking about his jeans without holes. The guy who's been trained puts the toilet seat down. And he signs your parents' birthday cards. So, the reason why a BBD isn't such a big thing for women as it is for men? Men want the pre-made statue of the Venus de Milo. Women want the clay to mold the man.

Lisa was introduced to the BBD when she asked her husband if he thought that his friend Paul was going to propose to Laura anytime soon. He paused and finally gave a response: "Paul's probably holding out to see if he can find something better." Lisa was a bit put off. Maybe put off is a little gentle. She was horrified! But in reality, some guys want to weigh their options before taking the plunge. Paul ended up proposing (eventually). But for his own peace of mind, he needed to first scope out the scenery. Then for the rest of his life he wouldn't be wondering what he might be missing.

THE GAME OF LOVE

Do you remember the '70s television game show *Let's Make a Deal*? My friend Dave wrote a story about what the game show would look like today. When I posted this on HisColdFeet.com, visitors replied with a lot of LOLs, so I thought I'd share it again:

You, sir, stand up. What's your name? Congratulations, Michael, and welcome to our show. We're going to start off by giving you $500 in cash. Here you go. I'll count it out for you. $100, $200, $300, $400, $500. Now, Michael, that $500 is yours to keep . . . or, if you'd like, you can trade it in for what's behind Curtain #2. What do you think, Michael?

Michael decided to trade the money for Curtain #2. Now, let me take that money back from you, Michael, thank you very much. And let's show Michael what he has won . . .

Michael, you've won a date with Mindy. Yes, she's a catch—she's smart, gorgeous, sweet, and she's funny. But, Michael, she may not be that perfect person you've been searching for. If you would like, you can trade in your date with Mindy for what's behind Curtain #3. Take your time, Michael, it's a big decision.

Ladies and gentlemen, Michael has chosen Curtain #3. Of course you did, Michael, because you're a man, and men are always wondering if there's something better out there. The Bigger Better Deal. So, Michael, you passed on a date with a wonderful woman hoping that you would find the perfect woman. The only problem is that she doesn't exist. But that's okay, because you're a man and there's something imprinted in your genetic coding that makes you unsatisfied with what is in front of you and leaves you longing for the BBD. So let's say good-bye to Mindy—'Bye, Mindy (the crowd joins in)—and let's open up Curtain #3, and Michael, you've won a date with . . . a mule. I'm sorry. But it's been fun. And thank you for joining us for another episode of Why Men Will Never Be Happy.

In a relationship, people may hit a pivotal point, where they consider if they're satisfied with what they have, or if they want to go for something that may be better. Of course people shouldn't settle, but what's important to distinguish is whether what they're ultimately searching for is a relationship that's a better fit or the BBD fantasy. It comes down to knowing if they're going after an image or a reality. Similar to the game show, the BBD can play on imagination, fantasy, and perhaps greed.

Your man wondering if there's someone else out there who may be more perfect has nothing to do with you. For you, just being in the loop about the BBD will help you with your own sanity, while also bringing him back to earth. The next time you pick up on the fact that your beau is holding out for perfection—pop in the DVD of *The Stepford Wives*. That should make him get over it real quick.

I was talking with a reporter for a Boston newspaper about guys not wanting to miss out just in case that perfect supermodel comes looking for them. She comically asked, "Who do these guys think they are? Brad Pitt?" Images can be perfect. But people are not.

Back in the day, my friends and I would go to these fund-raiser dances. That's how I met my husband, Joe. But that night Joe walked my friend home. And his best friend, Archie, took me home. After that, Archie never called. That was that. Then over the summer, a group of my brother's friends would run weekend dances up in the mountains for singles. I drove up with my brother and his friends, and right when we were pulling into the parking lot, Archie and Joe pull up right next to our car. At first, I was happy to see Archie. But he had wandering eyes. If he was with you he was always looking for someone else. And Joe was very attentive. That night Joe and I went for a walk,

we talked, and we sat outside on a blanket.
And that night Archie ended up alone.

—ROSE, 82, married to Joe for fifty-plus years

FORGET ABOUT FREEDOM

I'd have my freak-out moments about what I want
from life. It was less about [my girlfriend] and more about
me. I wanted kids and a family, but a side of me wanted to
grab my backpack and travel around the world. I was having a
tug-of-war in my mind with what to do.
I didn't want to give up my independence. Independence is
the biggest thing. That includes being able to do your own
thing, hang out with your buddies, etc. It took me a while
to get used to calling if I was going to be late.
I knew I wanted the same things as my girlfriend—a family, a
house. I just wasn't ready as fast. I wanted to be able to go
surfing when I wanted and biking when I wanted.

—RYAN, 34

Any man will tell you about how he got chills the first time he
asked his newly married bud to go to the Knicks game on a Saturday night and he responded, "Would love to, man, but gotta check
with the wife to see if we have plans." If your beau overhears this,
this is how he'll see his own future. The old ball and chain.

When guys talk about being afraid of losing their independence, I can't help but think that once married, both people lose a
piece of independence. Now they have each other to consider. It's
a gift that they're happy to give to their spouse. Unless you turn
into the crazy controlling Susie from HBO's *Curb Your Enthusiasm,* I can't help but think, "What's so terrible about two people
having each other?"

Sure, maybe no longer being on his own means good-bye to some of the bachelor-esque things he likes to do—no more coming home late without touching base with someone, no more trips to the bars with his buddies to check out the eye candy. But it also means someone to have dinner with, to cuddle up to, to bring him a bowl of chicken soup when he's fighting the flu.

Guys think once they tie the knot, they'll no longer have a say in how things go, or even what will be in the home. It's the tales of garage-bound armchairs, Goodwill boxes full of things that "don't go" with the rest of the décor, and sidewalks lined with life-size NFL cutouts on trash day. A friend of mine just moved in with his girlfriend. I asked him, "How did the move go?" He said, "Good, and she allowed a lot of my things to stay." He was one of the lucky few. For him, the fact that he was allowed to keep over 50 percent of his belongings made it a successful moving day. His things (posters, pictures, etc.) passed inspection.

On TV we always hear references to men wanting to get away from their wives. Just think about *Everybody Loves Raymond*'s Marie and Frank, Al and Peg Bundy, even the Mertzes. After picking up these messages, why would anyone want to sign up with someone whose job description of wife includes nagging them so much that they want to hide in the basement or garage? The bright side? At least they will be able to visit all of their things.

It's actually not you who he thinks will swoop away with his independence, pride, and dignity—it's marriage itself. If you let him know that you understand why guys would think this, it could lift a weight off his shoulders (a weight you can put in the garage with his barbells). How about showing him that with you he's signing up for something different? Let him know how much you love his baseball card collection. Make sure he knows his Thursday night poker games with the guys are a great time for you to meet up with the girls. Let him know that you expect him to continue to be himself. After all, that's the man you fell in love with.

A MAN IN GREEN TIGHTS

I thought getting married would take away the wonder of life. I was afraid it would be monotonous and boring. Everything would become a routine, and it just wouldn't be fun anymore. —DAVE, 38

To describe men who don't want to grow up, psychologist Dan Kiley coined the term "the Peter Pan Syndrome" and wrote the book *The Peter Pan Syndrome: Men Who Have Never Grown Up.*

Some men have shared that they don't want to get married just yet, because they don't want to give up some of the things they like to do. Putting off an engagement is a way to stop time, in a sense. If they get married, that means they're getting older. What they don't understand is that it's not like women don't want to defy aging. Think about all of the time-fighting creams and anti-aging serums in your beauty cabinet and makeup bag. We keep up on the latest research. We exercise. We rest. We get our antioxidants. Beyond creams and facials, men think putting off marriage keeps you young. Apparently, single men will never grow old.

Some guys also have an image in their mind of what a husband is like. Before tying the knot, they may feel they need to meet these expectations. Of course, that image is hopefully about being kind, respectful, and loving. But they're usually talking about something else. For most men, it comes down to money matters, as well as accomplishing a few other things before earning the title "husband." Some guys think they're supposed to have a certain amount of money in the bank, four suits in their closet, a nice family car, and a healthy 401(k) before they can get married and start a life with someone. Some think they're supposed to be completely responsible. And some, like Diana's boyfriend Jeff (chapter 2), think they're no longer allowed to order late-night pizza.

So there it is. Sometimes a guy is putting off popping the question, not because he's waiting for you to become something different, but because he's waiting for himself to become something different.

This makes sense, especially since I know plenty of women who are putting off having kids because they have a certain image in their mind of what they're supposed to be like and feel like before becoming a mom. They're waiting for that maternal instinct to kick in.

For these guys, they're living up to some pretty tough critics. Themselves. They may have an idea in their mind, but maturing into that ideal person doesn't happen overnight. Usually, it's a process—an evolution that takes time.

How about sharing with him some things that you feel are expected of you as a wife? Are you fearful of how you will be able to maintain a career and a household? Do you feel that you're expected to be Superwoman—clean, cook, raise the kids, take care of him, pay bills, run errands, stay in shape, etc.? After all, there's pressure for us to bring home the bacon and fry it up in a pan. Talking about your own expectations and the demons you're battling will help you to connect with each other.

Now discuss the expectations you have for each other. He doesn't have to own a luxury four-door. She doesn't have to make four-course gourmet meals every night. By talking this through, maybe he'll come to realize that the high standards he has set are just expectations he has for himself. At the very least, hopefully he'll understand that it is okay for a husband to order late-night pizza.

> The money thing isn't just an excuse. When the topic is money, a guy has a tremendous ego. It's hard for a man to look at his girlfriend and say, "I don't have enough money to get married." Money becomes an issue. —PHIL, 54

A TINY GOLD BAND, A BIG TRAP

> A guy has a lot of fears before he makes the decision to get engaged. I don't know if a guy wants to get married, but it's more like you resign yourself to the fact that you're going to have to get married. —JACK, 30

Some people look at retirement as life's finale. You've worked hard your entire adult life. So kick your feet up and relax. It's Miller Time. Long before this golden-year achievement, some men discover a different sort of "end." Marriage. They consider it a finale because that tiny band of gold makes them feel as if they're stuck forever.

It's not good to enter marriage nonchalantly with "There are no guarantees, so whatever happens, happens. And if it doesn't work out, I can leave." You shouldn't tie the knot with a slipknot. With that attitude you're not expecting much. On the other hand, it's not good to become mentally trapped either.

No one wants divorce. I had a conversation with a man who said, "Once I propose, that's it. No turning back. I don't want to ever get a divorce. So when I make the decision to get married, that's it for the rest of my life." This could work if he felt at peace with this. It was a sweet thing for him to say, but his thoughts on "no looking back and forever forward" were freaking him out even more. He felt like he was backing himself into a corner. It was like tying the knot was putting a lock on a door forever. Almost makes you feel claustrophobic just thinking about it.

After a little exploring he changed his way of thinking. He undid the lock and became more comfortable with a vow he made to himself: "I really don't ever want to get a divorce. I'm going to do my best to make this marriage a happy one. And when we hit an obstacle I'm going to give it all I've got to get through it. But if for whatever reason something happens at some point down the road and it's in both of our best interests to go separate ways to get to a better place, that will be okay." This perspective gave him a little breathing room, and he ended up proposing to his girlfriend soon thereafter.

If you're in a fabulous relationship, try to understand that it's not you per se that he's afraid of signing up with. It's his fears about life. With respect to change, guys seem to like to know the escape route just in case. Dare we acknowledge the fight-or-flight in all of us? If we can't fight, we want to know the way to fly.

When John moved to the suburbs, he kept his place in the city so he'd have somewhere to go in case his new home didn't work out. What if he didn't like the commute? What if it was too far from his friends? What if he missed the city? He decided he needed to hold on to his old place to help with the transition. So he signed a lease with a place across the bridge and continued to pay rent on his old one just in case he wanted to move back. Getting married is similar, except the escape route is a little trickier. Whether it's an apartment or getting married, guys feel safer making the transition knowing that if they're miserable they will have an option on where to go next.

NOT-SO-GREAT EXPECTATIONS

I thought that if we argued, that meant that she wasn't the right person for me. If we were right for each other, then we wouldn't argue over little things. I was also disappointed when I didn't feel the butterflies. If they weren't there, I was afraid I wasn't with the right person. —DAVE, 38

I have a friend who says, "I want to feel in love all the time." If he goes a little while without feeling the butterflies when he sees his girlfriend, he takes that to mean he's not in love anymore. While his girlfriend is waiting for him to propose, he's waiting to get the tingling feeling back in his belly. Was B. B. King right? Was the thrill gone?

His friends tell him, "No one feels in love all the time." They say people love all the time, but for the most part, the butterflies flutter to and fro.

Every day in our busy lives, we're surrounded by so many different emotions, stresses, and issues. Even things that don't affect us directly touch us personally. These can affect or put a damper on our emotions. From having a hectic day at work to a bickering battle with your BFF, these feelings pile on top of the "in love" ones. Sometimes it's tough to feel the excitement of love and adoration when you're just in a bad mood.

A friend of mine told me about a talk show she saw a few years ago. There was a guest on who sounded quite amazing. She was ninety-five years old and sitting next to her husband of seventy-five years. Imagine that. When the host asked her about their secret to a good marriage, the woman laughed, grabbed her husband's hand, and answered, "The trick is that we never fell out of love at the same time." See, the path to happiness isn't always lined with roses. There are thorns along the way too.

WHAT YOU SAID

In a survey, 118 people were asked if it's possible to feel "in love" all the time (some checked more than one response).

47 percent: You can love all the time, but you don't feel "in love" all the time.

27 percent: Yes, it is possible.

25 percent: No, not possible—the butterflies come and go.

3 percent: You only feel in love all the time during the honeymoon phase.

Here are a few of the responses from the 10 percent who checked "other."

I think that love changes as the relationship changes. The more you know about the person, the more things you fall in love with or learn to deal with. Love doesn't stay the same per se, but love is always developing. —GREG, 26

• • •

Love matures, so you aren't going to feel the butterflies as your relationship grows. What you get as you grow together and as separate individuals is absolutely amazing. It's an overwhelming feeling of unconditional love and support, which is the best you get in life. —TORI, 35

• • •

You can love someone but they can still drive you nuts.
—MONICA, 40

It's great to dream big. But when expectations fly off the charts, then that's when you can kiss any dream good-bye. I believe in setting high expectations, I really do. But when they're too high, it's almost as if you're setting yourself up for a letdown.

Then there are the misled few who think, "Marriage isn't supposed to be work at all." Who gave them this pearl of wisdom? You've heard that the best things are worth fighting for. Well, marriage is one of those things. The only thing that's a walk in the park is a walk in the park.

Most of the guys I know with unreachable expectations had parents who were "closet-conflicters." These parents never argued—so far as the kids knew. Once these men check in with their parents, they find out that, yes, their parents did argue. But by keeping their conflicts to themselves behind closed doors, they set an unreachable standard as to how a relationship is supposed to be. For these guys this means strolling down easy-breezy street, with no conflict.

When children of closet-conflicters have to deal with a disagreement in their own relationship, it's likely they'll take the conflict to mean that something's wrong: "My parents never argued. If it's a good relationship, this isn't supposed to happen."

If you have a suspicion that your boyfriend's parents are the type who kept it quiet (a prime example is a quizzically quiet holiday meal—no close family can get through one of those without a bicker or two), how about encouraging your beau to check in with the folks. They'll probably fill you both in. Ask them about what sorts of things they disagreed about and how they handled conflict.

BYE-BYE BACHELORHOOD

Men are used to different flavors of the month—bachelorhood is what they're used to living. All of a sudden they get bogged down for a year in a relationship, and it's not the flavor of the month. It's the only flavor. And they may

87

love that flavor and it's great and wonderful. But we know
that we better love this ice cream like it's the last ice cream
we're ever going to have. That's a little frightening. It's the
sense of "That's it." I think women have the opposite feeling.
They think, "This is a great person to get married to, so I want
to get married." I don't imagine they think right away, "How's
it going to be in five, ten, or fifteen years?" —CHARLIE, 33

Even though there comes a time in a man's life when he's out looking for Mrs. Right, there's something about the search and the conquest he'll miss once he finds her. On the search, men get to activate
their hunting technique—something they say feels natural to them.

There are two distinct sides to a guy. One side does eventually
want to settle down, but the other enjoys the thrill of meeting different women. (And you thought women could be two-faced!) It's
variety and adventure all wrapped into one. To some men, with
the first kiss as husband and wife, they're kissing bachelor days
and the chance of certain fantasies coming true good-bye.

Kevin Burke of the hit Broadway comedy *Defending the Caveman* sets these guys straight: "Relationships are not an Outward
Bound vacation. If you want to explore, take a safari." He reminds
men about what their hunting skills were for in the first place:
"Cavemen were hunters—so they could get food for their fami-
lies." In reference to the BBD, Kevin takes a more serious tone:
"There will always be someone a little sexier, a little smarter. But
with this you're setting yourself up to never commit."

No matter how unreal some guys' fantasies are, in their minds,
popping the question puts an end to any slice of hope there may
be for these fantasies to come true. Logically they know a fantasy
is a fantasy. But sometimes it's hard to admit that. It's like shutting
down the imagination he's had since puberty.

Think of it this way. We women are the target audience for bridal magazines, while guys are the target audience for another kind of magazine. Being bombarded with pictures like those on the cover of *Maxim, FHM,* and *Sports Illustrated*'s Swimsuit Issue, guys feel that once they tie the knot they're giving up a night with a Playboy bunny or two. Abandoning wishful thinking is another fear on the list of why not to get married right now.

Notes from the Professor, Dr. Judye Hess

I think it's often a harder decision for a guy to get married. He's going to move into this situation where he's responsible for a wife and kids, and he can't just go around and see different women whenever he feels like it. He's moving from a single guy into a husband, and that's a lot to lose. Whereas women, I don't think they're so socialized to feel "Oh, I have to give up seeing other men." They're usually happy to have this one person. That was their goal to begin with.

DIVORCE: A FOUR-LETTER WORD

My parents got divorced when I was very young. My aunts and uncles who split up were all married young. For me divorce was a common thing. Growing up, I had three friends from single-mom homes. I always wanted to get married, but I wanted to wait until it was right. I was going to be sure about it and not rush into anything.
I wanted it to last. —SETH, 36

Sometimes men (women too) feel afraid to get married because they watched their parents go through a rough divorce. When they consider entering a committed relationship, they see how the numbers are working against them. Most of all they're afraid of repeating a pattern they watched as a kid—the fighting, the bickering, the crying, and eventually the end of a marriage.

Children of divorce can go in two directions. They can become afraid of marriage and cynical about the legalities of binding a relationship. (Who can blame them? Marriage didn't work for their parents. And divorce was probably even worse.) Or, knowing their relationship can be fragile, they give it the extra care it needs. They feel excited about getting married and having children, because they feel cheated they didn't get to experience a strong family unit when they were growing up. They want to get to create that on their own.

If you believe your beau is postponing tying the knot because of his experience that marriage doesn't have a happily-ever-after, talk to him. Point out how your relationship is different from his parents'. If the main reason that he's holding back is because of his parents' divorce, he might find it helpful to talk to a counselor or therapist about this. Some couples find premarital or pre-engagement counseling helpful as well. This helps to get out the kinks in your relationship that are tying you up and holding you back. (See chapter 10 for tips on choosing the right counselor for you.)

COMMITMENT: QUESTION OR CONFLICT?

Although it's natural for us to take his hesitancy as rejection, most of what's going on is his very own battle with fear, change, the unknown, and learning the difference between reality and fantasy. All of which has very little to do with you personally.

So if you're wondering why your beau doesn't beam with enthusiasm when you bring up the *M*-word, maybe think about his

M worries—money, mother-in-law, my independence, etc. Hopefully you'll understand his struggle with the what-ifs. You're thinking happily-ever-after. He might be picturing giving up a guys' night to sit with you and your straggly unwashed hair in front of the TV eating bonbons and watching *Love Story* after yet another night with no action in the bedroom. Of course he "wants to talk about it later." Or at least once he can get this picture out of his mind. What does this come down to? That it's a guy thing. Just like with picking out different movies, women and men are dealing with different feelings when moving toward a marriage commitment.

Notes from the Professor, Dr. Judye Hess

More often women have issues around abandonment, and men have issues around engulfment. Each usually has some of each, but more often the guy is afraid he's going to be smothered. He's afraid that he won't have as many choices or he'll miss something in life if he decides to get married.

SHOW AND TELL

Here's what married men want to share with their nervous unattached counterparts. Goes to show that once a guy slays the pre-engagement jitters and gets the princess, he can look forward to making his home a castle—opportunity gained!

I was always afraid I'd wake up unhappy in five years. Years later, I got married. I'd say allow yourself to be happy and live in the moment. Every day we wake up and make choices about how we are going to live our lives . . . Don't think too

much about the future. Be present and enjoy the amazing
feeling of having a partner in your life. —ANDY, 32

. . .

Once I came to realize that we wanted the same things but
she just wanted them sooner, it was okay. She had a mental
plan that she wanted to be pregnant by thirty. And now, four
years later, we have a one-year-old son. It's what I always
wanted in life. We have a house by the beach so I can do all
the stuff I like to do. I'm not being stopped from doing it.
Now I'm just sharing it with my family.
Early on, part of me thought about the BBD. I'm sure she did
also. You have to be comfortable in the fact of knowing
you're going to meet other people too. You're going to meet
women and think, "She's so hot and cool." But for me, at
the end of the day, I really love the person I'm with. You have
to be okay that in life you're going to meet other people
you're into. The scene was fun, but by the time I got married
I was so over it. —REX, 34

WHAT YOU SAID

One hundred and fifteen women and men were asked what
they thought was the top fear that men deal with when it comes to
getting engaged. In other words, what makes him want to put off
proposing to his long-term girlfriend? (They could choose more
than one reason listed.)

56 percent: Fear of losing his independence and freedom
44 percent: The what-ifs
41 percent: He gets scared thinking about settling down with
one woman for the rest of his life
24 percent: He's wondering about the Bigger Better Deal

22 percent: Doesn't want to say good-bye to bachelorhood
20 percent: If he hasn't proposed, he's just not ready—it's as simple as that
20 percent: Fear of getting divorced

Some responses from the 17 percent who checked "other."

A lot of men don't trust themselves to be able to commit. We know how we think, and we don't think about one woman forever. So it's really about fear. I'm afraid I'm not good enough to be a husband. —WILLIAM, 32

• • •

Hasn't found the perfect mate. —LILLY, 58

• • •

A wife, in general, is more difficult to live with than another guy friend or living alone. Marriage is a double-edged sword, and men have a difficult time seeing, much less understanding, all of the positive things that come with a happy and successful marriage. The positive things are not well advertised to most bachelors. —ETHAN, 37

• • •

Fear of change/the unknown. Why change something that isn't broken? —PATRICIA, 28

• • •

My husband constantly heard from his friends that everything changes when you get married . . . as if the girlfriend suddenly turns into a monster once she becomes a wife. His friends would say, "My wife was soooo cool when we were dating, and once we got married, everything changed!" —ZOE, 32

Guys need to be assured their life isn't going to change
that much. —PHIL, 54

HIS "JUST BECAUSE"

Realizing that in general guys don't feel ready to get engaged as
quickly as women do is a little gem of information you probably
forget when you're wondering, "Where's my diamond?" It seems
so easy for everyone else, right? After all, you've got a half dozen
weddings to go to this spring. You can't help but think all your
friends landed a clone of Prince Charming. Her boyfriend swept
her off her feet, so what's wrong with yours?

You've heard from some guys that they'd like to put off marriage for as long as they possibly can. On that note—you know
that after struggling to get to "I do," many guys come around. You
want to know, "What makes him do so?" So I asked men, "What
made you feel ready to propose? What does 'ready' feel like?"

Here's my report: Seems they have the same problem narrow-
ing down concrete reasons. Some say it's "just a feeling." How frus-
tratingly vague. Still others say they'll feel ready when they stop
struggling with the doubt, the fear, the racing heartbeat, the sleep-
less nights. Sounds like it's about feeling content with the decision
you're making.

I learned that a guy is apt to pop the question when his relationship has its "mojo." When a relationship is in a slump, no one's
going to think, "This is the perfect time to get engaged." When
you're in relationship funk (bickering over who left the dirty
dishes in the sink, how he forgot to take out the garbage, and how
he wasn't friendly enough over the phone when he wished your
mother a happy birthday), this is how he pictures your life

together as a married couple. Marriage becomes a world of nagging, being told what to do, and being talked at, not to. Who wants to be first in line for that?

I know this gets tricky. It's almost like a catch-22. When you want to get engaged and he's dragging his cold feet, you're ticked off! You get frustrated! You're mad at him for making you go through this! How can your relationship not be in a slump? And every time you get one of those cutesy bridal shower invites from someone who's been dating her beau for way less time than you've been in your relationship—the tension builds.

Apparently someone forgot to tell him, "When the woman of the house is happy—everyone's happy." You want to know, "What am I supposed to do? I'm hurt! I'm mad! And I don't feel good about myself!" It's important that you don't deny yourself your feelings. And definitely don't fake a happy face to sprinkle some of that relationship mojo in the air. The idea isn't to cover up how you really feel. Instead, try not to let his keeping a proposal from you seep into your entire relationship and well-being. More importantly, don't allow the fact that he hasn't proposed yet make you feel bad about yourself. Remember, it's not about you. It's about his own process. Easier said than done, right? We can make it easier done . . .

Acknowledge your feelings. Find someone you can talk to. A friend. A counselor. A family member. You're probably holding a lot back (hence the mini-explosions). Some exploring and venting will help clear out the feelings. In doing so, you'll discover that this isn't about him rejecting or not accepting you—but about how you want to get engaged and he doesn't (right now). He's struggling with his own issues and may just need time to sort them out. In the meantime, you're probably hearing, "Can we talk about it later?"

5

His Love Affair with Later: Putting Off the Talk

She needs to make herself clear.
She should remember, she's
negotiating.
—PHIL, 54

Maybe you've been dating for a year, or two, or three, or more . . . and now you find yourself on the other side of "dating dodgeball."

You made it through the first round—parents and friends chasing after you asking if there's a ring in the near future. Now you're in Round 2. But this time the tables have turned and you're the one asking, "So when do you think we'll get engaged?" and it's your man who's bobbing and weaving: "I don't know. Hey, gotta run."

You're trying to get information about your future together, and he's giving you zero to work with. You're about to throw your hands up in the air. It's frustrating trying to pull (or should I say yank) answers out of him. But your road to His and Hers has been stymied by His vs. Hers and your differences in how you approach things. Many guys define the *M*-word as "Maybe-later."

The other night my husband and I went for a walk along the water near where we live. It was beautiful out. No fog. Clear views of the Bay Area. It was gorgeous. We're walking, I'm talking, talking, yapping, and talking some more—when I got a glimpse of my husband's face. He had this expression that looked like he just wanted to stop in his tracks and take a load off. That load would be me.

You see, I was overloading him. He wanted to just walk, enjoy being outside, and take in the fresh air. I didn't think about it that way. All I knew was that when I take a walk with a girlfriend we talk. If we didn't talk, it would feel awkward. I'd think, "Uh-oh, we have nothing to talk about. Are we growing apart?" Girlfriends talk the whole way. We fill every little step up with words. I didn't realize there was any other way.

So for the rest of our stroll we tried his way. We walked. We took in the scenery. It's not like we were playing "let's see who can go ten minutes without speaking first" (although he initiates that one in the car sometimes). Sure, every so often one of us would comment about the architecture, the scenery. And it was really nice. I felt like I was introduced to something new—a new way of being. Boy, was it relaxing.

Since women tend to be an interesting (okay, confusing) combination of being emotional and analytical by nature, it's only natural for us to want to translate his "I don't knows" and "can we talk about it laters." Our imaginations take hold and away we go. We analyze and analyze.

Not only are we looking for the deeper meaning behind his responses, but we also want to know how to get past the dead end. Because when he says "I don't know" it feels like just that—a dead end, a road to nowhere.

However, "I don't know" can be simple. Maybe he honestly doesn't know. Perhaps he has some stuff to figure out. Before he can answer to you, he has to answer to himself. To identify if this is the case, ask yourself: Does he generally get freaked out when talking about the *M*-word, or is it possible he genuinely doesn't know how he feels about getting engaged right now?

Whether it's early in the relationship ("Where do you see this going?") or three years down the road ("Why aren't we there yet?"), men seem to get a little jumpy talking about marriage. It used to be all cute and quirky how he would squirm, but lately it's not even remotely endearing how he bounces from "Let's talk about it later" to "I'm just not ready" back to "Let's talk about it later" followed by "I don't know." This is an all too familiar routine, and it's getting old.

When I went through limbo, I quickly picked up that my boyfriend's "Can we talk about it later?" response was in direct relation to how often I'd ask, "What's taking so long?" Somehow during our relationship and the issue of engagement, he had decided that dodging became a sort of trouble-free safety zone. So the more I asked, the more he wouldn't answer. We could be anywhere. Doing anything. And the question would slip from my lips. On the way to a friend's wedding, "What about us . . . ?" While reading the morning paper and spotting a diamond ring ad, "When do you think . . . ?" I was one to preach about the importance of boundaries and giving people their space. Was I now a hypocrite? Before my nondefensive communication technique kicked in (we'll talk more about this in chapter 7), my reaction to his "I don't knows" would make things worse. I'd ask. He'd answer. I'd react (with a harumph), "Well, fine, then!" Then we'd end up talking about it for hours. So whenever he wasn't up for another go-around, dodging the question seemed like the most logical thing to do.

It wasn't long before I made a deal with myself: "Okay, I'm going to go three weeks without bringing up marriage." I was prepared. I even had friends lined up to be on call. My instructions: When I felt the urge to bring up engagement, I would speed-dial one of the girls instead. Great plan. And it would have been an even better plan if it had actually worked! Truth be told, I failed a few times before successfully getting through three weeks in a row marriage-chat-free.

BECAUSE NO MEANS NO

When you've exhausted yourself asking him why he keeps avoiding the topic, it's common for you to start bugging your friends: "Why does he keep avoiding this?" The answer to this question should be obvious, but sometimes it's not. It's simple math. We bring up marriage because we're ready. He doesn't bring it up because he's not ready.

To understand more of what goes on behind the curtain (you know, the one your beau keeps hiding behind), I asked my husband for the lowdown. He said quite plainly, "If a guy was ready to get engaged, he would have done something about it already. If women are trying to decipher what 'Can we talk about it later?' stands for—it means, 'I don't want to talk about this.' Right away a guy knows if a conversation starts with 'When do you think we'll get engaged?' it isn't going to be pretty." Guys think that if they choose to engage (in the conversation, that is), it's not going to go anywhere. Or even worse, it could lead to tears. So why jump head-first into the fire when you can cuddle by the fireplace in silence?

Even though we're married now, my husband still quickly changes the station as soon as he hears the local jeweler's voice on the radio: "Show her how much you love her with a diamond ring from . . ." I think he gets flashbacks.

WHAT THEY SAID

Here are a few responses from the guys as to why men want to "talk about it later" when marriage-minded Chatty Cathys want to talk about engagement:

He's not in touch with his feelings, or doesn't have the language/vocabulary to talk about the complex feelings that may arise. He may not want to hurt his girlfriend's feelings by talking blatantly about the struggles of monogamy, etc. —ANDREW, 40

• • •

It destroys the spontaneity if you talk about it, then he proposes. A lot of the excitement is sucked out of the situation. —LAWRENCE, 39

• • •

Discussion equals planning the event and moving forward. —ALEXANDER, 28

HIS LIPS ARE SEALED

Anytime you ask a guy to do anything that isn't pleasant for him, whether it's taking out the trash or unloading the dishwasher, he's going to say, "Not now, I'll do it later." He wants to put off things he deems to be unpleasant for as long as possible—until he has to do them. —Jack, 30

If he keeps dodging what you want to know, try changing what you ask. Asking him, "When, and why not now?" makes him feel like he's supposed to have an exact answer—a date, a time, even the play-by-play. And he doesn't. I bet even if he did, you wouldn't want him to shout out, "August 15!"

My friend Eileen was the kind of kid who searched for birthday presents. When her parents went to sleep and she knew they had just done some shopping, she would sneak around and find the wrapped gifts. She would never open them, though. She just wanted to know they were there, that they were on their way to her, not necessarily what they were. This translated into her adult life and her own engagement limbo conversations.

> I would talk to Jay and ask him over and over and over
> again when it was going to happen. One time, he turned to me
> and said, "Do you want to know when it's going to happen?
> Because I'll tell you." I immediately stopped talking.
> I didn't ask him again for a while. I realized that being that close
> to finding out the surprise was too close for comfort.
> So I backed off. I was going to get what I wanted . . . to
> find out when we were going to get engaged. But I
> realized that I didn't want to know the exact time.
> That wouldn't be any fun! —EILEEN, 34

Here's a breakdown of what he hears when you pop your own question.

"When" implies you want to get a date down on the calendar—now. In pen.

"Do you" aims the question directly at him. Only him. There's nowhere to hide.

"Want" puts the pressure on him to agree that's what he wants, when maybe it's not.

"To get engaged"—there goes the blood pressure. Just the word itself ups the stress.

He's been dodging your questions, and you don't want him to start dodging you because he's starting to feel pressured. Instead of dropping questions on him (which only frustrates you more), let him know what's on your mind. Give him a little prep time—let him know what you want to check in about. Not only will it take the pressure off him for opening up more, it'll lift the frustration from you. It's a win-win.

When we ask, "When do you think we'll get engaged?" we have an expectation as to how we want him to respond. He can't read your mind, and chances are he won't give you the answer you're looking for. Not yet, at least. If he could, you'd have a ring on your finger. So how about taking a step back? And instead of directing a question at him—let him know that you want to chat about something that's a tough topic. Since you're not at ease talking about this either, let him know it's scary for you too. Together, agree that if something comes up that hurts one another's feelings, you'll let each other know. Expressing feelings doesn't have to equal arguing. Try to talk about how you each feel so you can both get an idea as to where you stand. (Look for more communication techniques in chapter 7.)

Here's how to get started:

"I'd love it if we could check in with each other about our thoughts on our future." From there, he has time to breathe. He knows you aren't going to corner him. This will be a safe discussion, not a barrage of questions thrown at him with an unbearable force.

Some advice from a couple of guys on how a woman could bring up engagement to her boyfriend:

In all honesty, when he says "I don't know what I want," he probably doesn't mean "I don't know whether or not I want to get married." He means "I don't know whether or not I want to get married to you. And I haven't figured it out yet. The reason why I haven't figured it out is that it's not an issue for me right now, so I haven't given it any thought. So I couldn't possibly have that conversation with you right now." To break through this avoidance, she has to put him to the decision. She says, "I understand that you're not ready to talk about that now. You need some time or whatever. I'd like you to think about it." Then she should make a reservation at a restaurant for a month from that day, and say to him, "We're going to talk about it then." She should put a time frame to discuss it. Not an ultimatum, but a time to discuss it. If he doesn't take her seriously and he doesn't talk to her about it at that point, then she needs to rethink things. —JACK, 30

• • •

You don't want to give him an ultimatum—but at the same time you want to get questions about your future answered. The main thing to remember is that you don't want to just rip the Band-Aid off the guy. —CHARLIE, 33

If you read John Gray's book *Men Are from Mars, Women Are from Venus*, you probably picked up on how men are problem-solvers and women are talkers. Ask him something that involves a solution, and he's in. "Honey, I'm having a problem with the garage door . . ." When there's a problem with a solution, then he's ready to talk. Put him on the spot with something he can't solve, like "When do you think we'll get engaged?" and it's likely you'll get nothing.

Lucy told me how she reacted to the news of a colleague's engagement. "When Terri got engaged, I started wondering why my own boyfriend hadn't proposed yet. I asked him if he saw us getting married. He reassured me that he did. So I asked, 'Well, then, how come we're not engaged yet?' He said, 'I want to get married, and I want to marry you. But I feel like I just want to keep hitting the snooze button.'" Is it just as desirable for guys to hit snooze on tying the knot as it is for us to hit snooze when we want a little more beauty rest?

Wondering why all guys don't explain their take as straight-up as Lucy's boyfriend? There's always the fear of rocking the boat, baby—just as he doesn't want to tell you how he really feels about your mom, he doesn't really want to have to tell you why he's dragging his feet. What if it starts an argument? What if it hurts your feelings? What if it leads to hours and hours of circling around the topic or tears?

As we read in chapter 4, men have all sorts of what-ifs. They also have their fantasies. This may be one of the potential reasons they don't want to put a ring on your finger. A peek inside a guy's mind: "What if the new hot girl at work is supposed to really be the one? She seems perfect." To be fair, maybe a guy wants to keep these thoughts in strict confidence. Let's be realistic. Is he really going to say, "I'm not ready to get engaged because part of me wants to see if the woman in accounting is more perfect for me"? Guys keep their lips sealed. Smart move. (However, in chapter 6 you'll find ways to break through this.)

But remember, the men haven't cornered the market on this one, ladies. Is this any different than when, in the strictest confidence, one woman fesses up to another that she always thought she'd end up with someone who was more of a professional or more outgoing or—gasp—better-looking?

There are certain questions that guys know they shouldn't dare touch. "Do these jeans make me look fat?" "How did you like the dinner I made?" "Isn't our waitress pretty?" These are known as setups. Their friends warn, "Dude, don't answer that." When he thinks you'll get engaged is on this list. Because if he hasn't proposed by the time you've wanted him to, he knows no matter how he answers your question, it's not going to be good.

For example:

Donna: So, when do you think we'll get engaged?
Dan: ["Uh-oh, here we go again . . . What's safe . . . ? What's safe . . . ?"] I don't know?
Donna: What do you think?
Dan: ["Uh-oh, uh-oh . . ."] Don't know. I'm really not sure.
Donna: Do you see us getting engaged this year?
Dan: ["Okay . . . here we go . . ."] Well, I'm not sure. [Deep breath] I think there are a few things we need to work on before—
Donna: Like what? You don't think our relationship is good the way it is?
Dan: I'm just trying to say—
Donna: I hear you! Fine, then! Never mind. [Door slams.]

Before asking why he's not ready, consider whether you really want to hear the answer. Because if you get angry with him for opening up, it will be forever programmed into his mind that talking about engagement equals an argument. But stay true to yourself too. If he says something that makes you mad, this doesn't mean take it so he'll continue sharing. No way. There's a healthy balance to sharing in this situation. Since tension and defensiveness can easily fill the air when talking marriage, laying down some playground rules beforehand may help smooth things out.

Remember what Robert Fulghum taught us in his book *All I Really Need to Know I Learned in Kindergarten?* Tie your hair up in some ribbons and follow these three simple rules that can be applied to engagement:

1. Share.
2. Be nice.
3. Listen.

A key point to remember is that women and men communicate differently. Just look at how many books there are on the topic. Professors dedicate years of research to studying gender communication—at home, in the workplace, etc. It can come down simply to how we're socialized. Women make plans to get together to talk and catch up. Men make plans with each other to play basketball. We're talking. They're doing. Our differences can especially catch up with us when we're talking about our relationships. Sometimes his expressing why he's not ready yet can be as difficult as it is for you to stop the VCR clock from blinking 12:00.

> Women are constantly wanting to check in on how their relationship is going, while men just want to be in the relationship. —CHARLIE, 33

WHEN DESPERATE TIMES . . .

One woman was so tired of her boyfriend taking flight every time she tried to talk to him about their future together that she gave

Scott Lorenz, balloonist and president of Westwind Balloon Co. in Michigan, a call. Scott shared this story: "The main point of the flight was for her to corner her boyfriend in the balloon basket and flat-out ask him about their future together. She explained that she was very frustrated that every time she brought it up he walked out of the room. He'd say they'd talk about it later, etc. She wanted the answer now because she wanted to get married, and if he wasn't interested in having kids she was moving on. It was a desperate thing for her to do, but it was pretty creative. He couldn't leave the balloon basket—not at five hundred feet off the ground."

When I asked guys the best way to break through the brick wall and curb the "I don't knows" and "talk about it laters," no one actually mentioned a balloon ride, but they did have some good insights.

> She has to have a practical reason as to why the status quo is not the most desirable situation. If there's no practical reason to change things, then—no matter how cliché—the guy is going to say, "Things are going great. There's no reason to rush into anything. I don't want to screw things up." Also, guys think the reason she wants to get engaged is because she wants to start a family. If he wants to have kids too, then that's great. But typically the guy's not going to be ready to have kids as early as his girlfriend. It becomes a negotiation. Basically, there has got to be a reason, other than just "I think we should get married." There's got to be some practical reason to get married. Or it's inertia. —JACK, 30
>
> • • •
>
> She should try to present that she's ready in a way that's not threatening, not confrontational. She should make

it more about trying to understand what the big things are that he's concerned about, and she needs to figure out if the two of them have the same long-term goals. Their time frames might not be the same, but the plan needs to be the same. —RYAN, 34

Just as I asked men what's the best way for a woman to approach this conversation, maybe you can ask your beau what he thinks will help him get past giving three-to-five-word responses. What does he need to help him open up a little more? With this approach, maybe you can give him what he needs to help him give you what you need.

WHEN TO ZIP IT

Ever notice that "How are you?" immediately triggers "Good, how are you?" Ever notice how shocking it is when someone actually gives you a real answer instead? Keep asking your beau when you're getting engaged or when he's going to be ready, and you'll get the same habitual response, "I don't know." Not only that, but it's like the passenger in the backseat who asks, "Are we there yet? Are we there yet?" The car ride goes that much slower for everyone involved. Asking "Why not now?" can actually decelerate the speed of his process.

If you can't keep yourself from bringing it up, it might mean that you could use a little space from the *M*-word yourself. What would it be like to put the issue aside for a bit, so you can enjoy your relationship for what it is? Don't put a hold on the issue indefinitely, but consider what's a reasonable amount of time for you to go without discussing it. Does a month feel okay? If this is a relatively new issue in your relationship, does four months feel right?

No need to keep this self-imposed hiatus a secret. Let him know that you realize the two of you aren't in the same place on your feelings, so you're giving him a breather from talking marriage so he can figure it out. Think of this conversation as a preliminary chat. Remember, the goal isn't to get him to come rushing home with flowers and a diamond to ask you to marry him. The goal is for him to think about what's going on and why he keeps dodging the question. Is he afraid of saying the wrong thing, or does he really just not know? This is the time for him to proactively get in touch with himself, rather than buy more time.

Keep in mind that if he doesn't want to talk about it, then he's probably not in the best place to express his feelings right now on this one anyway. But if his "I don't knows" and "can we talk about it laters" seem to be a pattern that constantly repeats itself—tell him what you're noticing, and together figure out what you need to do to get past this dance so you can move on to something else already.

ENTER AT YOUR OWN PACE

I get e-mails from women who ask, "If the guy hasn't brought up engagement, how far into the relationship is a reasonable amount of time for the woman to bring up their future as a couple?" When I surveyed women and men on how far into the relationship the M-word should come up, responses were varied. Some women said six months, while some men said three years. However, most agreed that it depended on the couple, the quality of the relationship, and their ages.

> I think it depends on their ages and their plan. If they're young and have time, maybe they should let the relationship run its course. But if they're a little older or already in their thirties, perhaps sooner. —EMILY, 31

. . .

> This is not a matter of how many months or years. It's up to the individuals to decide. —ANA, 67

. . .

> Depends on the quality of the relationship.
> —MARK, 33

. . .

> If either person in the relationship has gotten any clues from the other that this relationship isn't going in the direction they choose—it's time to have the chat. —JEAN, 61

Regardless of the time frame you decide on, just like marriage, pre-engagement is about meeting in the middle. I was talking with a woman who said, "If both people want the relationship to work, maybe it means that he'll have to get married a little sooner than he would have liked, and she'll have to get married a little later than she would have liked." Well put!

Notes from the Professor, Dr. Judye Hess

The more someone in a relationship pursues, the more the other person will distance. It becomes a dynamic where the woman starts to ask [about marriage] and the man feels pressured and engulfed and backs away more, then she advances more. It turns into a power struggle. He doesn't want to give in if he feels like it's her idea. He thinks, "If I go through with it, then I'm giving her what she wants." She thinks, "Why shouldn't I have what I want? I should go for it."

6

The Chat: How to Talk the Talk (Finally!)

It's the minority of guys who want
to settle down and bring up
marriage first.
—SETH, 36

WHAT'S YOUR STYLE?

It isn't a new concept. The driving force behind any good relationship is good communication. You need it to figure out if you're meeting at the gate, baggage claim, or curbside pickup. Whether he's getting the dry cleaning or you are. Imagine how important it is to talk effectively if the conversation is about something uncomfortable and emotional—like being in pre-engagement limbo.

A starting point for good communication is to identify your own style. How do you approach issues? What is your typical tone of voice? Do you ask questions or bark accusations?

Let's look at which type best describes yours. Then you will learn how to work your strengths and avoid your weaknesses for a more successful (and productive) chat with your man.

QUIZ

1. You're watching celebrity weddings on the E! channel. You:
   a. Shout to your boyfriend in the next room, "When are we going to get engaged?"
   b. Pout to yourself, "When am I going to have my own wedding feature?!"
   c. Say, "Honey, this is called romance . . . repeat after me . . . ro-mance."

2. You're on vacation having a romantic sunset dinner and you:
   a. Say, "This would have been the most perfect place for you to propose."
   b. Hold back tears because the couple at the next table just got engaged and now the entire restaurant is ahhh-ing.
   c. Say, "I'll have the diamond ring," when the waiter asks what you would like for dessert.

3. When your beau asks how your day was, you say:
   a. "Great. And by the way, do you remember meeting Linda from my office? Well, she wants to know when we're getting engaged."
   b. "Fine," and then slink to your room in tears because you dodged three people who asked, "Is there a big day coming up soon?"
   c. "Do you see a ring on my finger? No? Well, then I had a crappy day, didn't I?"

Picked mostly A's? You're probably the Speak-Your-Mind kind. Connected mostly with B's? Then you seem to be the Save-It-'til-Later Communicator. Do the C's sound like you? Perhaps you're

Sarcastically Sassy. Selected one of each? Your style, like your fashion sense, changes with your mood.

YOU'RE A SPEAK-YOUR-MIND

Strengths: One thing for sure, people know what you're thinking. No questions there! You wear your heart on your sleeve, on your pants leg, and on the strap of your trendy bag. Knowing what you want and when you want it is an amazing trait that shows strong conviction and self-worth—a gem that's hard to find.

Weaknesses: Your assertiveness can be seen as aggressive at times, which can often scare people off. Jumping out at people can put them on the spot.

You and your beau are out for a casual lunch. You ask him to pass the salt and pepper. He hands them over, and "Thank you" is replaced with "So when do you think we'll get engaged?"

It's great to be inquisitive, but keep in mind, even mentioning marriage probably scares the be-gee-bees out of him. Dropping it on him like a piano from the sky anytime, anywhere, only leaves him unprepared and flattened. He'll probably find it difficult to express himself on the spot, which will only frustrate you more.

The fact that you always say what's on your mind is one of the things that he loves about you. But if he clams up at the mention of marriage, perhaps he's afraid of saying the wrong thing. Then you're 0 to 60 in 8.4 seconds and the argument begins.

To approach your man with the best intentions, try starting the conversation like this: "I've been thinking, and I would love it if we could set aside some time to share how we each see our relationship growing. That way we can make sure we're on the same page."

Setting aside a time to talk lets you both come prepared for the chat. You wouldn't want to walk into an important office meeting unprepared, so why would a talk about your future be any different?

By setting a chat date (at least you're setting a date for something!) both of you will have some space beforehand to gather your thoughts about what you want to say and how you want to say it. Then you'll be able to share your fears, ideals, and expectations on getting engaged while giving each other the space to be honest.

YOU'RE A SAVE-IT-'TIL-LATER COMMUNICATOR

Strengths: A cool cucumber, you know there's a time and a place for everything. You don't let emotions take over, and you put time into your thoughts and explanations.

Weaknesses: Burying real feelings can come back to haunt you, not only through overemotional outbursts later on but as physical ailments. Avoiding heartache now could give you a stomachache later.

When you get upset, do you tend to hold in your feelings for as long as you possibly can? Do you put on an act pretending that everything's okay—then eventually (usually around 2:00 A.M.) your feelings pour out uncontrollably? After lying in bed for hours, eyes open in the dark, tossing and turning, you give your beau a little nudge to make sure he's still up. If he's not, too bad . . . he's up now! You ask, "Can we talk?" but what you really mean is "We're talking." Suddenly you're knee-deep in a conversation that lasts longer than the movie *Gone with the Wind.* Pillow talk quickly becomes pillow yell. The sun pops over the horizon, everyone's eyes are red, and it's off to work you both go, without anything resolved.

We've all done it—sometimes we hold in our feelings until we're ready to explode, and then, at the most inappropriate time (either at bedtime before lights-out or minutes before the door opens and friends pour in for a dinner party) we do. But why do we wait to share our thoughts? Is it because we don't feel entitled to our feelings? Are we embarrassed to talk about them in the moment? Do we need time to realize what we're angry about, or to find the right words? Maybe we're trying to stick to our New Year's resolution of not sweating the small stuff.

While some of us feel more comfortable planning what we're going to say, keep in mind that this strategy does have its downsides. One: When you hold off too long sharing how you feel about a situation, your boyfriend may not even remember what you're talking about. In his mind, the moment in question has already passed without incident. Since nothing was mentioned at the time, he thinks everything is groovy. An argument later on is like getting rear-ended in a parked car.

Two: While you're waiting for the right time to talk, you might think you're perfectly composed, but to an outside eye, you're tense. You're probably holding onto anger and it's seeping out in other ways (like snapping at him for leaving his clothes on the floor). Shoving your feelings under the carpet can get messy, and it can start to cause some bumps in your relationship. And don't forget, he knows you. He knows your left eyebrow goes up when you're annoyed. He knows when something is bothering you by the way you call him by his first and middle names. He knows something's up when you pick at him. The question he has is what.

What would happen if you tried to share how you feel closer to the moment of when you get upset? There might be a place and time for everything, but it's still possible to say something gracefully in the moment. The wording may not be perfect, but the release and feelings will be authentic. It'll be difficult at first if you're not used to doing this, but the more you do it the more natural it will become.

I was a Save-It-'til-Later. I used to struggle to say what I felt, until someone once said, "Whatever's bothering you—it's how you feel and that's okay. Feelings aren't right or wrong." From that point on it got easier. Those words combined with a lesson on "I statements" set me in the right direction.

In Professor Judye Hess's class we learned that "I statements" are ways of explaining your feelings without blaming anyone else for making you feel them. "I statements" don't cause the listener to become defensive and can make conversations easier and more productive.

An example of an "I statement": Chloe tells her boyfriend, "I was hurt because I felt like you spent the whole night talking to your ex-girlfriend at Jake's party." Robert responds with, "Oh, I didn't realize."

If Chloe hadn't used an "I statement," the conversation might have gone differently: Chloe says, "You spent the whole night at Jake's party talking to your ex-girlfriend. Why don't you marry her?" Robert would then probably respond with something like "You're crazy, we talked for fifteen minutes" or "What, now I can't talk to other girls?" Just a slight change in the phrasing can make all the difference.

YOU'RE SARCASTICALLY SASSY

Strengths: The comeback queen, you have a witty sense of humor that helps you tackle tough times, as well as keep people entertained and always laughing. You're quick on your feet.

Weaknesses: Sarcasm can hurt. A sharp wit can sometimes cut. Also, sarcasm tends to hide the true meaning of things and can be misconstrued if it's too vague. Being sarcastic leaves what you really mean up to interpretation.

Cracking jokes and making sarcastic remarks are much easier than expressing how you really feel. When talking to your beau, the sarcastic you might say, "The good news is that at the rate we're going, we'll get a senior citizen discount off our wedding venue."

Sarcasm is a defense mechanism—pure and simple. Although you've got some clever lines (amateur night at the local comedy club, here you come), there's a serious downside to your funny business. When you don't say exactly what you mean, it can be difficult for your boyfriend to understand how you really feel. He's left decoding messages—and there's no guarantee he'll ever get the hidden meaning. There's also the chance that sarcasm will create a distance between you two, because he won't realize how seriously to take your feelings. And in return you won't feel understood.

Next time you're about to reach for that fabulous one-liner or that well-thought-out dig, think to yourself what you really want to say. If you want him to know it's hard for you to move forward because you still don't know where you stand on your commitment, then say just that. The more you practice saying what you mean, the easier it gets.

Don't get me wrong. He loves your witty sense of humor, and no one's suggesting that you trade in those quirky hits for dry and boring. Just realize that even though sarcasm comes easily for you, it may be counterproductive to a serious conversation about feelings, fears, and other difficult topics. People need to feel safe before they can open up and let themselves be vulnerable. If you're using a defense mechanism such as sarcasm to protect yourself, he may use another defense mechanism, such as avoidance or denial, to protect himself.

YOU'RE THE BEST OF THE BEST

One night while watching *Sex and the City,* my friend Kim filled me in on something she just heard: "The different personality types of Carrie, Samantha, Charlotte, and Miranda are supposed to portray that of one woman." And so it goes with all of these communication styles I've described. We all have a piece of each characteristic in our personality. Sometimes we're feeling sarcastic, sometimes we're more direct, and sometimes we'd just rather hold it in. What's important is understanding each type, how it hurts, how it helps, and how to make it work for you.

WHAT'S HIS TYPE?

Just as women have different conversation styles and defense mechanisms, so do the guys. As with heights, weights, and favorite sports, each man has a different way he acts and reacts when approaching a discussion topic. Once you identify his MO, you can figure out how to work with it. Identifying how your man communicates will allow you to pick up cues so you can get your message across in a nonthreatening way.

Which one of these best describes your beau?

QUIZ

1. *You ask him about when you two are going to get married. He:*
   a. Says, "I really want to get married, but I'm just not sure when."
   b. Says, "Can we talk about it later?"
   c. Gets annoyed that you're even bringing it up.

2. *You tell him news about Dana and John's engagement. He:*
   a. Seems really happy and then later freaks out because as

long as John hadn't proposed he was somewhat off the hook.

b. Runs into the other room and starts downloading songs onto his iPod (and one of them isn't the "Wedding March").

c. Says, "That's because Dana let John propose on his own."

3. *You've just had a talk about marriage and now:*

a. You're more confused than ever. Did he say he wanted to get engaged, or did he say he didn't?

b. You realize you actually didn't talk about it because he kept changing the subject.

c. You're upset because your beau ended the conversation with "The wedding is your thing, the engagement should be my thing."

Answered mostly A's? He's probably a Fickle Fred. Picked mostly B's? Although he works out like the Terminator, he's actually the Procrastinator. Went with mostly C's? You're in love with Mr. Me.

DEALING WITH FICKLE FRED

Your boyfriend talks about how much he wants to get married. You've covered it all: how many kids you each want, whether there's a dog in the picture, if you'll stay on the West Coast or move back east. The talk gets your mind going—in fact, you're already perusing TheKnot.com, and you have one glass-slippered foot in the dressmaker's shop. But then, out of the something-borrowed-something-blue, he gets scared and clams up, and you might as well forget about Googling "destination wedding."

It's a roller coaster. One minute his eyes are watering during

Ellie and Barry's wedding ceremony, and within an hour after the cake cutting, he's as white as the frosting. The good news is that you don't need to worry about putting any pressure on him; he's doing the dirty work for you. We can all be our own worst enemy. Fickle Fred does a fine job of freaking himself out without your even saying a word. Guys can be excited about the prospect of settling down, but they can also become nervous about it. What they haven't realized is that being nervous is part of the game. It's normal and it's okay. With this guy, it's important to know how to talk to him when he's in the panic mode. A good technique for this is called "Naming," a way to let him know the things you notice. Consider it an Eye Spy game, but you're spying with your little eye actions, not items.

Here's an example of Naming: "It seems that you can get excited about the idea of getting married, but then you also get pretty freaked out too." (Nothing gets past you!) Also tell him that since you two talk about all the fun things that come with marriage, you're hoping you can share what feels scary about it as well. This is a great time to share your own fears about being married. After all, this is a major change in both of your lives. It's scary! He'll feel at ease if you tell him what freaks you out.

One of the struggles for guys is that when they're about to get engaged, they think they're supposed to feel a certain way—joyful, happy, excited. Usually a mix of emotions comes up—including getting freaked out. If you two can talk about what feelings are coming and going, then you can get through this stage together.

DEALING WITH THE PROCRASTINATOR

Every time you try to talk to him about rings and things, he tries to buy more time. You're tired of hearing the range of "Can we talk about it later?" to "I don't know." You feel shut out. Not only do you have zero idea of his overall thoughts on engagement, you don't seem to ever get a chance to talk to him about it. The Naming technique used with Mr. Fickle also works well in this case. Once again, this reflects to him what you see in a nonconfrontational way.

Here's an example: "I notice every time I bring up getting engaged, it's really hard for you to talk about it." To make sure that the conversation doesn't shift into the "Can we talk about it later?" phase, try continuing with this: "I know that talking about getting engaged can be scary, but I think it's important for us to each share how we feel. It doesn't have to be right now, but I'd love it if we could pick a time to sit down together and share how we each feel about the next phase of our relationship."

If you're afraid he'll show up to this date with more "I don't knows" and "maybe laters," try asking what it is that he needs to be able to get in touch with his stance on the *M*-word. Even though men are explorers by nature, they usually aren't too eager to explore this aspect of tying the knot.

DEALING WITH MR. ME

Would you say your beau is hooked on the idea of surprising you with the ring? Is he traditional in thinking it's up to the man to decide when to pop the question? You try to talk to him and he says, "It's up to me to surprise you." By this point, you're thinking, "Buddy, you snooze, you lose."

These types of guys can be pretty set in their ways. Whenever you bring it up, he adds four months to the proposal (he'll show you for butting into a man's place!). Whether it was through his family, friends, or society, this man was trained to think everyone has his or her own job—he lands the engagement, then you plan the wedding.

Talk to him about how this affects you. Let him know that on one hand you understand that he wants the proposal to be a surprise and you'd enjoy that too—but what's even more important for you right now is to be able to talk to him about his thoughts and when he imagines getting engaged.

Some guys will say, "I want it to be a surprise" or "I want to make sure I'm really proposing because I want to, and not because I feel pressured." If you want the proposal to be a surprise, but it's still important for you to know his time schedule, have a chat about that. If he's "married" to getting around to it on his own time—how about checking in on what time that is? It would be nice to know it's sometime before your iPod becomes obsolete.

STUCK IN COMMUNICATION LIMBO

It's not news that men find it tough to discuss commitment with their girlfriends. There was even a TV commercial about this oh-so-painful act of sharing. As a test of strength, a man dons a padded suit, goggles, and a helmet and sits down . . . to talk to his girlfriend about their future together. He only lasts five seconds, until he has to be pulled out and resuscitated with a beer.

It doesn't have to be this way. Talks can be easier than you think. But they take work. And a keen eye. Start to pay attention to the communication patterns that come up for you as a couple by asking yourself these questions:

1. **Do you bicker?** When you hold back your frustration, whether you want to or not, it'll find a way to come out. It might manifest itself in the most ridiculous ways. You may be triggered by going to someone else's wedding, and that night you actually end up in an argument about

how he never puts the cap on the toothpaste. If you're constantly bickering, this usually means you haven't faced what's really upsetting you. Bickering is a way of masking real issues. Use this information to help you understand that there may be something else in your relationship that needs addressing.

2. **Do your conversations about marriage go nowhere?** If this is the case, you may be holding back how you both honestly feel about the subject. You may be tiptoeing around instead of getting to the heart of the matter. Perhaps you're trying to be accommodating. You don't want to be pushy or have an awkward conversation, so at the first sign of conflict you back down. The key thing to remember is that there is a conflict. You want one thing, and he wants something else. In fact, this is true on many levels. You want to talk about your future together, and he doesn't. You want an honest answer of whether he plans on marrying you in the reasonable future, and he doesn't want to give you one. You want to get married now, and he wants to wait. This is conflict. But things don't have to get ugly. You do, however, have to be able to tell him how you really feel: "I know that talking about getting engaged can be a really tough conversation to have, but it's important that we share how we each feel so we make sure we're on the same page."

3. **Do you each take things you say to each other too personally?** She says, "I feel ready to get engaged," and he translates that into, "You're a big jerk because you can't give me what I need." He says, "I'm afraid of making a mistake," and she hears, "I'm afraid that marrying you is a mistake."

As much as guys flip the remote during commercials (who knows . . . maybe something better is on another station), I've also heard them say "I'm afraid of making a mistake" when someone flips the topic to marriage. There's also the popular "What if someone else is out there who might be more perfect?" You can chalk these up as guy things, and they probably have nothing to do with you personally. When you start to open up to share how you each feel, it's important to try to let the other person have his or her experience.

Since men aren't on the fast and eager track to talk about anything wedding-related, the key to breaking through their walls is to let them know that you "get it"—you know it's a tough conversation to have, and it's even harder for guys. This way they'll feel that you understand them and that you're on their side. To keep him from shutting down, watch your tone. Understand; don't condescend.

Our communication styles are a good indicator of how we actually feel. Recognizing our patterns helps the chat move past the "I don't knows" and can curb our dropping those daily hints— subtle or otherwise. Ultimately, this helps us get through the limbo rather than have the limbo take over the relationship. In the next chapter, you'll find out how to keep the talk going once you get him to open up.

7

Once He Opens Up

It really worked for us to sit down and for me
to explain that this isn't a conversation either
one of us wants to have, but it has to be had.
I told him that if there's something he feels he
wants to prepare so I'm not catching him off
guard, we can write stuff down. I wanted us to
at least go into this talk feeling comfortable.
He absolutely responded to when I told him I
didn't want to have this conversation either. It
made him feel more at ease.
—STEPHANIE, 38

Waiting for a proposal can get the best of you. And
sometimes you can't help yourself. There seems to be
a gravitational pull toward the topic. Subliminal hints
during dinner. Bridal magazines "accidentally" left on the coffee
table. Local jeweler's trunk-show invites in his lunch bag. Subliminal? Not really.

In this case, it's quality over quantity. One good talk is better
than a hundred vague mentions. But it's not a good idea to spring
it on him. Don't catch him off guard during a football game or
while he's putting on his tie for work. Instead, set aside a time
with your partner to talk about this next phase of your relationship. Have an open conversation and honestly express your feelings and concerns. Being direct about your feelings is most

effective. Passively dropping hints will only cause you to circle around the topic, making it more difficult to tackle the issue. It's okay to get right to the heart of it. Getting engaged is about both of you.

Once you've finally broken through his silence and his "can we talk about it laters," he'll be a bit more willing to talk. Now that you've got him to open up, there are ways to make sure he doesn't clam up.

NOT YOUR AVERAGE TEA

I read in my welcome packet at the counseling center where I did my graduate school training, "T-Group will be from 6:00 P.M. to 7:30 P.M. every Wednesday." How nice, I thought to myself. I had a lovely image of all of us trainees sitting around sipping tea and talking about our feelings. In actuality, T-Groups aren't as relaxing as they sound, but I do credit them for getting me through my relationship flux.

The *T* in T-Group didn't represent cozy chamomile; instead it had to do with training, specifically nondefensive communication training. Sounds like a complicated tactic, but it's really quite simple. I picked up that nondefensive communication goes like this: You tell them how you feel, they listen without getting defensive, then they respond nondefensively while expressing their feelings. Sounds like a perfect world.

So we were talking about our feelings, like I originally thought, minus the hot beverages. These group chats were an opportunity to share with our peers something they did to tick us off, or something they did that we appreciated. Here's an example of this type of chat:

JaneDoe: Can I T with you?

Andrea: Okay.

JaneDoe: I notice lately that I've been getting annoyed when you show up late to the class we're in together. I felt really irritated today, because I was giving a presentation and I felt interrupted and distracted when the door opened. I felt angry when I lost my place and had to start over from the beginning.

(Note: The nonmaster T-er might want to respond, "Maybe if you knew your presentation material better, a squeak from a door opening wouldn't throw you off." But that would be defensive. It's better to let JaneDoe have her experience instead.)

Andrea: Jane, I'm glad you're sharing with me how you feel. And, I feel bad that you were distracted during your speech . . .

I had a love/hate relationship with the T's. They were draining and hard, but necessary lessons on communicating. I definitely wasn't looking forward to 6:00 P.M. on Wednesdays. Every time I heard, "Andrea . . . ?" my shoulders would clench up to my ears and I'd quickly scan my memories for what I could have done to upset someone over the last week. But after graduation I actually missed them. Whether I realized it or not, I was bringing T-Group home. It was peeking into my relationship with my beau. Nondefensive communication helped me talk about my pre-engagement drama as we were going through it. With time, I was soon listening to him talk about his fears, his what-ifs, and his ideals about getting engaged without reacting or getting defensive. I was actually—gasp—listening. It helped me to learn and to understand him better. Of course, our chats didn't always feel good. Sometimes it stung to hear a laundry list of reasons why he wasn't ready to get engaged. But this list gave me insight into my relationship. Warm fuzzies aren't always the end result of a good, honest chat.

Deciding to be in the loop of what your partner's thinking and feeling is a personal choice. This down-and-dirty dance with honesty can be a case of "Careful what you wish for, because you just might get it." If you ask to hear what someone's feeling, you should be prepared to hear the good, the bad, and the ugly—all with a nondefensive ear. Decide if you want to hear what your partner honestly has to say. In my case, I wanted to hear everything. All the nitty-gritty. I guess you could say I wanted to hold the sugar and take my tea strong. After all, the only way we could grow together and improve our relationship was if we shared our expectations and fears.

At the end of the semester I walked away from T-Group with these insights:

1. It's important to let people have their own experiences.
2. I shouldn't get hysterical if someone tells me I've upset them.
3. I should get in better touch with my own feelings.

There's another lesson to be learned from this type of communication. It's not for everyone all the time. You might want to show off your new technique like your latest shoe purchase, but not all people will appreciate your up-front feelings. Nondefensive communication can actually turn the tables—people can get defensive if they don't know what you're doing or if a T is sprung on them.

Sharing in this up-front manner isn't the norm. People tend to sugarcoat things, ignore them, or keep things to themselves. (If you don't have something nice to say . . .) And let's face it, it can be sort of disconcerting for people to hear what you think and how their actions make you feel. So once again, timing becomes everything. Although you're encouraged to share your feelings, and it feels stellar doing so, it's important to first explain where you're coming from.

SHARE AND TELL

How you approach someone is important. If you decide to begin a conversation with "When are we going to get engaged?" you better hide his running shoes. Start instead with "I'd love for us to share how we each feel about getting engaged."

Men don't talk as much as women do. Just look around at a restaurant. Ever notice how at the tables for two, it looks like the women are doing most of the talking? Or when your man makes plans with his buddies, it's rare that they get together to chat. Cheer on a football team together, yes. But talk about feelings, not so much.

So one of the biggest differences is our communication styles: We want to talk about it. They don't. Let's take a listen to how women and men handle conflict in their own ways.

Scenario 1: Rachel calls Deb for a bitch session about something that Lori did (and said) at a meeting at work.

After thirty minutes of giving Deb the lowdown, Rachel asks, "Can you believe Lori?"

Deb gets even more into it, complete with supporting side

comments. ". . . she did what?" A peacemaker at heart, Deb eventually asks, "Do you think you can talk to her about this?"

Rachel: "I don't know. I mean, can you believe her?"

A few days go by and Rachel's still fuming. Knowing she can't avoid Lori forever, she calls her. "Can we talk?"

A talk like this isn't brief. It's a "she said, she said" session. Going over details and feelings. Then going over details and feelings again.

Scenario 2: Rich is ticked off at his coworker/buddy Doug because he feels that he's telling him what to do during an important project.

Rich: Dude, you're being a jerk.
Doug: Sorry, man.

And back to business.

That's it. That's all. No hour-long phone calls going back and forth on who said what and how they said it.

Guys seem to tell each other how they feel when they feel it. Briefly.

So if you're frustrated because your conversation on "feelings" is going nowhere, be a little more patient and try to see it from his side of the court. You may have had more practice at talking things out.

Since men don't get as much talk time, talking about intimate things can be intimidating for some (at least until they get more practice). Since women both talk and share well, we can adjust to let them know we want to *share* our feelings rather than *talk about* them. Sharing. Now you're speaking their language. Guys feel like they can share. Whether it's a six-pack of beer during Monday

Night Football or a b-ball on the court during a pickup game, guys get practice at sharing.

SETTING THE TABLE

Here are a few ways to make the talk successful and comfortable for all parties.

1. You and your beau set aside a time to share how you both feel about getting engaged. You decide together what you'll share: feelings, hopes, expectations, and dreams. If it helps, make an actual outline on paper or index cards, so that you won't stray into different topics than the one at hand. It'll help you stay focused.
2. Pick a place that's comfortable for you both—for some that might mean on the cozy living room couch, or while taking a walk together. Any place that feels relaxing and distraction-free will do. If you don't live together, choose a neutral location. If you'd feel safer having someone there to facilitate, perhaps consider discussing your feelings in couples therapy. (See chapter 10 for tips on finding a therapist.)
3. Remember this is a chat during which you'll share your feelings. Steer clear of blaming and judging. Listen to each other.
4. Sharing lets you in on how the other feels about getting engaged, so that you can open up about your fears, expectations, and hopes.

NO FUSS DISCUSS

Wendy and Mark have been dating for three and a half years and have been living together for the past two. They have a close

ONCE HE OPENS UP

relationship, and the main issue right now is that Wendy wants to get engaged and Mark wants more time. Sound familiar? For the past year it has been a tense topic, and when they do talk about it, Wendy feels the conversation doesn't lead to anything. They decide they're going to chat on Sunday morning. They're sitting on the couch with their feet up on the coffee table, and Wendy begins.

She says, "I've just been feeling really sad that our relationship seems to be so stuck. I feel confused because I know that I love you and I want to continue to grow with you. I really do want to be as patient as I can, but at the same time I know I want to get married. I have my own limits as to how long I can wait before finding out if we want the same things."

Wendy shares her experience. Without giving an ultimatum, she lets Mark know that putting off their engagement isn't sitting well with her. She's simply sharing her feelings without asking for anything from him in return.

Mark says, "I know I want to get married, and I want to marry you. I'm just having a tough time because I always thought that when I'd propose I'd feel like there was no turning back. I feel really scared, so I think that means that the timing isn't right yet."

Mark begins to open up and is starting to admit to feeling scared about proposing.

Wendy says, "I know that getting engaged can be scarier for guys. I mean, just think about the look on Adam's face right before he got married. I'd love it if we could talk about what you feel scared about so we can see if there's anything about our relationship we need to work on."

Wendy is letting Mark know that she understands. She brings up how nervous Adam looked, to help add some levity to the discussion, as well as bringing a sense of normalcy and camaraderie to Mark's feelings.

As they continue to talk, Mark tells Wendy that his fears stem from the actual concept of getting married. He talks about "What if it doesn't work?" and other possible scenarios. For Mark, venting these fears and frustrations starts to alleviate the pressures. Wendy begins to understand Mark's fears a little better, and Mark feels more comfortable knowing that he can talk without being punished for his honesty (sometimes hard to take). He knows that she's not pressuring him to get married, but at the same time understands that it's unrealistic and unfair to think she will wait around forever. They begin to feel a little closer, decide to try to enjoy their relationship for the time being, and agree to check back in three weeks to see where they each are with things.

EVERYDAY CHATS

No matter who you talk to (relationship counselors, your mom, couples married for fifty years), they'll always say that what gets a relationship through the tough times is communication. It will help you in every stage of the relationship, not just in deciding when to get married. Being able to open up with your partner and talk is more important than having a crazy sex life, a big bank account, or looking perfect in every photo you take together. One time in a relationship where good communication is vital is when you're learning to live together. Or should I say learning to live with each other—because after all, you don't just marry his family, you marry his habits too.

During a few chats about engagement, other issues might rear their ugly heads. You will probably talk about your beau's fears about getting engaged, but you might also end up discussing his fears about you. This is where it can get personal.

We all have habits that drive our loved ones insane. Some find it ridiculous that their significant other can't seem to replace an empty toilet paper roll (actually putting it on the holder). Others don't understand why it's so difficult to ask for directions. And what's up with the random open cupboards—why can't they close the door after they get a coffee cup out? I find that when it comes to things that bug us about each other, women and men react differently.

For a great example, let's visit Julie and Bobby's home on a Sunday morning. Julie's on her way out the door to run some errands. Panicked energy fills the air as Bobby watches her storm around their apartment searching for her wallet. She looks under *The New York Times,* which is scattered all over the coffee table. She shuffles through large coat pockets and tote bags. She mumbles to herself, "Where is it?" as she opens and closes the closet doors. Bobby's not alarmed. He just shakes his head from side to side and knows that no one is on a shopping spree with Julie's credit card. This happens all the time, and her wallet always shows up. Somewhere in his mind, Bobby might decide to turn this typical trait into a reason for alarm. "Why is she so disorganized? How am I going to live the rest of my life with someone who can never find her wallet, her keys . . ."

That's right, our bad habits freak men out. Women seem to have a greater tolerance for men's annoying habits. Guys extrapolate into the future and think about what it will be like to spend the rest of their lives dealing with our bad habits. Bobby's not thinking, "Oh, that's just Julie."

No matter who it is, there will always be some things about a person that bug us or trigger us. For some people, annoying habits are deal breakers, because they can't imagine their partner ever changing. However, letting your partner know what it is that's pushing your buttons is where to start for some change.

For instance, Julie doesn't enjoy misplacing things. In fact, it drives her crazy too. It could help her if Bobby brought it to her attention and offered suggestions to help her try to overcome this flaw. "I just hate watching you get completely crazed when you're looking for your keys. Why don't you try keeping your wallet and keys in the same place, so you'll always know where they are?" Just keep in mind, there are always areas in a relationship that can use some improving. The only way issues can get worked through is if couples discuss what they are.

FAQ

Question: I've been dating my boyfriend for a little more than two years. I need a few pointers with things. When I try to talk to him about getting engaged, he shuts down.

Answer: Guys tend to get jumpy or shut down altogether when they hear the *M*-word. An opening like this can help: "I know that talking about getting engaged can be scary, but I feel it's important that we're able to talk about this." When you let a guy know that you understand it's a tough conversation to have, he feels like you get it and you're on his side.

Question: I usually have a hard time talking about my feelings in general. I keep a journal because it's much easier for me to write down how I feel. My boyfriend is the same way. He writes music and expresses his emotions better that way. Is there somehow we can use this type of communication to our advantage in terms of talking about our future?

Answer: If it's easier for you to express your feelings by writing, then by all means, grab a pen and get to it! You and your beau can set aside a time to have a writing session, where you each write about how you feel about getting engaged. Remember, you're writing about your feelings, not using your pen like a sword. You could write a letter sharing your hopes and fears. When you're done you can either read the letters out loud or, if it's more comfortable, read each other's silently. This is a great way to let each other know where you stand and can also be a good bridge to opening up the lines of communication.

Question: My boyfriend and I are both divorced. I'm forty-two and he's forty-four. We've been dating for more than a year, and I have felt ready to get engaged for a while now. How can I bring this up and talk to him without pressuring him or being pushy?

Answer: There's a big difference between sharing with your boyfriend how you feel and pressuring him. Find out how he feels about getting married again. Try starting with "We've been dating for a while now. I thought it would be good if we shared with each other our thoughts about marriage and our feelings about where we each see this relationship going." This is very different from "All our friends are married, and everyone is asking why we aren't engaged yet! I'm expecting a ring by my birthday." Getting engaged is about both of you. It makes sense that you want to make sure you're on the same page. Talking about your hopes, expectations, and fears about getting engaged doesn't have to be a pressure cooker. It's a way to find out if you both want the same things and have the same agenda.

QUICK TIPS ON TALKING ABOUT GETTING ENGAGED

Get it: Let your guy know you understand that talking about getting engaged can be nerve-racking. He'll feel like you're on his side. How to say it: "I know that talking about engagement and marriage can be scary . . ."

Stay curious: If he might as well be speaking Greek, ask him to translate. He says, "I'm just afraid that things will change." How to respond: "What are you afraid will change?"

Use "I statements": Try to share how you feel rather than focusing on the actual timetable of what's taking him so long to propose. How to say it: "I'm having a really tough time because I feel ready to get engaged, and I don't fully understand how you feel about this."

Avoid daily digs: Wow, is it tempting. But bringing up a wedding or engagement whenever it's on your mind isn't the best way to go—especially since it's probably always on your mind. When you feel you need to talk about it, let him know. Dropping hints or nasty digs will only make him shut down more.

Try not to take everything he says personally: If he decides to open up and share his thoughts about his fear of making a mistake, or even if he brings up the Bigger Better Deal—keep in mind this doesn't have to do with you personally. On the flip side, if something he says is hurtful, tell him how his statement made you feel. You can also teach him about "I statements," so that his feelings will be easier for you to hear.

What helps and what doesn't, from those who have been there:

> From the guy's perspective, he never wants to talk about getting married—until he's independently made a decision that that's the way to go. A good time to have the chat cannot be measured by the calendar. It depends on the situation. —JACK, 30
>
> • • •
>
> If she pressures him, it only pushes him further away.
> —CHARLIE, 33
>
> • • •
>
> Bringing it up several times a day definitely didn't help my relationship. —LISA, 33
>
> • • •
>
> What helps to get through this is communication and patience. It's important for each person to be open about how they feel. Really try to understand where the other is coming from. What didn't help us was friends and family constantly asking what the deal is. Whenever someone asked us "when," we always ended up arguing about that. —ANDY, 32

SHE SAYS/HE HEARS, AND WHAT SHE REALLY MEANS

She says:	What's taking you so long to propose?
He hears:	What's wrong with you?
What she means:	I'm ready to get engaged, and I'm having a hard time waiting to find out where you stand on this.

She says: Everyone we know is engaged.

He hears: Blah blah blah.

What she means: Why aren't we engaged yet? It's impor-
                   tant that we're on the same page. I feel
                   that for my age and our time together,
                   this means getting engaged.

HE SAYS/SHE HEARS, AND WHAT HE REALLY MEANS

He says: I'm afraid of making a mistake.

She hears: Marrying you is a mistake.

What he means: I'm afraid of what will happen if we don't
                   get along in ten years.

He says: I want it to be right when I ask you.

She hears: I don't want to marry you, because we're
                   not right for each other.

What he means: This is important to me, and I want to
                   make sure it's a special proposal. I have
                   my ideas of what I want to do, and I
                   want to do it that way.

GUY CHAT: A MAN'S PERSPECTIVE

The goal of the talk is to learn the truth. That's it. But it's
important to remember that if a guy feels like he's going to
get punished for sharing his feelings, he won't share them.
Hearing how he really feels might be tough, but it's always
better to know the truth.

Getting him to open up will be difficult at first, since he's
programmed to only tell you good things ("You don't look
fat." "You're prettier than our waitress.") and to steer away

from any potential conflict. To undo what's been done, you may even need to prompt him by explaining that you're in it for the honesty. Once you get him going, he may open up, and you should be prepared for what he might say, even if that something hurts. He's afraid that there's someone better for him out there. He's afraid he doesn't make enough money. He's afraid sex will get boring. He's afraid he won't be able to spend time with his friends. He's afraid it might not work out.

These things may be difficult to hear, so make sure you want to hear the truth before you embark on this journey. Remember that the goal is just to learn where you stand. With that information you'll be empowered to create your own destiny, instead of waiting around to let someone else choose it for you. —DAVE, 38

8

She Proposes, She Proposes Not

I think that if I proposed, I would
regret it the second it came out
of my mouth. I'd always wonder if
it was something that he would
have done. If he said yes, I'd
wonder if it was because of
pressure. And I think I'd be
hostile toward him for not
proposing first.
—STEPHANIE, 28

THE GIRLS CHASE THE BOYS

I always get a kick out of the responses from people when they hear about the concept of "His Cold Feet." I just say the words "His Cold Feet," and suddenly it's the topic of dinner conversation. If those at the table aren't going through pre-engagement limbo themselves right now, they either did before they got married or know someone who has. For the single girls in the group, chances are they have a friend who's going through it. And before I know it, I'm getting scoop upon scoop on people's sisters, friends of friends, and sisters of friends of friends.

Whenever this topic gets going, inevitably someone asks, "Why doesn't she just ask him to marry her?" Genius! The most logical solution is right in front of our eyes. You're dating a guy. You want to get engaged. He hasn't proposed yet. Ask him yourself. It's just so simple. My thoughts exactly.

When I did some digging, I realized not too many women felt this way. At least not when it came time to put their proposals where their mouths were. When both people know they want to get engaged, what keeps her from proposing? Pride? Is it the wrinkles she fears she'll get in her dress if she were to get down on one knee? I thought I'd know more women who proposed, but I could barely find a few. In fact, I had to travel back in time to find a land where the women took charge of the marriage proposal, or at least once a year they did. I went to a place called Dogpatch, U.S.A.

Li'l Abner, known as the greatest comic strip of all time, was created in 1934 by cartoonist Al Capp. It told tales of a small town as seen through the eyes of a lovable character, Li'l Abner. Dedicated fans from all over the country followed his trials and tribulations until 1977. The strip, filled with satire and humor, played on gender issues as well as political and social ones. Readers followed along as the gorgeous Daisy Mae spent two decades chasing Li'l Abner in the Sadie Hawkins Day race (an event where the women propose to the men) so she could marry him. He kept running, and running, and finally Daisy Mae caught Li'l Abner. The wedding bells rang out in 1952, an event that got national attention—their story graced the cover of *Life* magazine.

SADIE HAWKINS DAY

Sadie Hawkins Day, a day when the women take the wheel and drive the men to the altar, left a mark on calendars and on the programs of school dances. This concept of women taking the more masculine role of choosing, chasing, and proposing to a mate addressed serious gender roles in a light, more approachable manner. The relationship between Li'l Abner and the frustrated Daisy Mae really resonated with people of all ages.

From *The Old Farmer's Almanac* at Almanac.com:

> Not a typical holiday, Sadie Hawkins Day was the invention of Al Capp, creator of the Li'l Abner cartoon strip. Capp conceived of a day in Dogpatch, U.S.A., when all the unmarried ladies could pursue (literally) their men. If caught, the hapless bachelors were soon trudging down the aisle. This fictional world so captured people's imaginations that Sadie Hawkins Day passed into the realm of modern folklore. The first Sadie Hawkins Day took place in November 1938. Today, it's usually celebrated on a Saturday in early November to accommodate all the girls-ask-boys school dances and other events.

I spoke with Caitlin Manning, Al Capp's granddaughter and a documentary filmmaker and professor of film at California State University–Monterey Bay. I asked her about the strip, its characters, and the magnificent influence it had on our society. During our time together, whenever Caitlin referred to the adored Li'l Abner, she could have been talking about any number of guys I know today. It was truly life imitating art.

Caitlin explains: "In *Li'l Abner* the girls are trying to get the guys, and certain guys are trying to escape. Li'l Abner, for example, wants to be free and he doesn't want to have any attachments or responsibilities. The character resonates today—there's the male fantasy of freedom and being free of obligations."

It seems that even back in good ol' Dogpatch, U.S.A., the men didn't pop the question before women got the engagement itch. "In the strip it's the women who are the domesticators and have to capture the men and bring them into family life," says Caitlin.

It turns out that even the sexy character, Daisy Mae, shared similar thoughts with women who go through pre-engagement limbo today. Caitlin continues: "Daisy Mae, who is in love with Li'l Abner for years, asks why he won't marry her. She thinks maybe she's not pretty enough and wonders how she can make herself adequate enough to get the guy. The comic strip implies that it's not in a man's nature to want to get married. They need the women to make it happen."

And in the case of Sadie Hawkins Day, that means, ladies, lace up your running shoes. It's time to physically rein your men in. This notion goes hand in hand with the traditional idea that, back then, women were the fabric that held the family together. This was just another stride she had to take toward creating a family unit.

"There's a certain mythology surrounding engagement and proposals that's challenged through Sadie Hawkins Day," says Caitlin. The myth it's debunking is that of a strong man getting down on one knee and, with steady words, proposing to his beloved. In reality, the picture isn't very sexy—it might be a man who is shaking like a leaf, can't find his voice, drops the ring, and fumbles the Big Question.

So the main thing to ponder becomes, is the image of the perfect proposal a myth? And instead, is the reality a guy with trepidations? Caitlin says, "It wouldn't be considered romantic to show the guy being wimpy about it. Guys don't want to be bachelors all their life; they just need a little push. They don't think of the benefits of marriage. Sadie Hawkins Day clearly encourages a certain practice. The practice of women chasing after the guys was okay—no shame, no guilt, just part of the mating ritual."

And Caitlin has no shame about saying that she proposed to her husband. "I was the one who was much quicker to be ready to get married," she says. "In my family it was all girls—so we weren't compared to men in terms of what we were or weren't expected to do." So she just told the man she loved straightforwardly, "Let's get married." And they did . . . happily.

A PICTURE OF TREPIDATION

I was so nervous as I was driving to pick up the engagement ring that I slammed into the back of a lady's car and caused her bumper to fall off in the middle of a busy street. Since the engagement ring was so expensive, I was too scared to tell my car insurance company for fear my rates would increase. I couldn't afford high monthly payments on a ring and higher insurance rates, so I just wrote the lady a check for her expenses and never reported the accident. Hey, no one was hurt. That was twenty-three years ago. Erin and I made it through that little crisis. We've been happily married since. –BRAD, 47

THE RESULTS ARE IN

Only recently as we flip through the TV channels or the pages of *People*, we're starting to hear more women asking, "Will you marry me?" There's the all-time favorite *Friends* episode when Monica initiates the proposal to Chandler. Pop singer Pink popped the question to her boyfriend—and it made huge news! Even watching the ladies call the shots on the TV reality show *The Bachelorette* empowered women from their living rooms.

To find the fact among the fiction, I went in search of real-life characters who had proposed. In a survey, I asked 118 people:

1. How many women do you know personally who proposed to their boyfriends?
2. How many weddings have you been to?

Much to my surprise, knowing women who proposed wasn't as common as I thought it would be.

75 percent: knew 0
20 percent: knew 1
3 percent: knew 2
2 percent: knew 3

And a couple of people checked "other"—they were wondering if giving a guy heavy pressure counts as her proposing.

Anyway, there were only thirty-eight (assuming that respondents weren't referring to the same bride) brides-to-be popping the question out of a total of more than 1,634 weddings this group attended.

Women seem to be waiting it out instead of popping the question themselves. The question now is, why? As such a small group, the women who did propose became all the more intriguing, like a small group of rare beautiful butterflies. I wanted to know what made them decide to do so.

I also discovered that it's easier to hypothetically say, "Yes, I'd propose," then to actually do it. At least I know for myself that's true. Today I'd say, "Absolutely I'd propose myself." But would I have done it when I had the real chance? No. I believe it was my attachment to thinking that things were supposed to be one way or another. This was how I was trained: Send a thank-you note within two weeks of receiving a gift. Don't wear white shoes after Labor Day. And in this case, he's supposed to propose. But my advice for any girlfriend would have been to go for it! How empowering it would be! Back then I just couldn't walk the walk. A walk that could have led me down the aisle a lot sooner.

WHAT YOU SAID

I posed a question on HisColdFeet.com: "Would you propose to your boyfriend? Why or why not?" From all the submissions, there were a few women who wrote, "I did propose." The number of replies that answered "yes, I would" or "no, I would not" were pretty much even.

For those who said, "Yes, I'd propose"—here are some of their comments:

"Women need to take control of their life."
"Sometimes men need a little push."
"At least by proposing you'll find out where you stand."
"Absolutely! You think he's going to wear the pants? I'm going to show him who's boss up front."

For those who said, "No, I wouldn't propose"—here's what they had to say:

"I'd always wonder if he really wanted to get married."
"I know he's not ready. Proposing would only guilt him into it, or make him feel pressured."
"I'm a hopeless romantic."
"I'm too old-fashioned."
"I've always dreamed of being proposed to."
"I want him to show me that he really cares."

WHAT STOPS THE POP?

Aside from girlhood dreams and old-fashioned ways, most women say they hesitate to propose because they'd be left wondering if he really wanted to get married in the first place. After all, if he really wanted to, then he would have asked himself, right?

Responses are all individual, but for some women who proposed, they know that they're the "planner" in the relationship—vacations, paying bills on time, getting together with friends. They feel that if they don't plan it, then it's not going to happen. The same with making dinner and picking up a movie—they don't plan it, it doesn't get done, and they're left eating mac and cheese from a big bowl staring at a turned-off TV. Some women feel this is just the dynamic of their relationship. Since he won't initiate dinner with friends, these women don't think their boyfriends would initiate something as big as marriage. Some say, "I didn't want to wait, and I felt like it was the right thing to do." Others take the surprise approach, using a proposal as a way to step out of character and do something thrilling that they both will never forget—the ultimate surprise!

I more or less proposed to my boyfriend, because I knew he
wouldn't be the one to do it since he's one of the shyest
people I know. Something along the lines of proposing
wouldn't be something he'd initiate. He didn't even initiate
the dating. I end up taking the lead.

I wanted to get married, and I was comfortable talking
to him about this because I felt our relationship was ready
for the beginning of the rest of our lives. I knew if I didn't bring
it up, it wouldn't be brought up, and it was tearing me up
inside. I had trouble sleeping until I finally let him know that
I wanted to spend the rest of my life with him and that I
loved him with all my heart.

After that we started planning our wedding, deciding on the
style, who to invite, etc. Then on New Year's Eve he officially
proposed to me. —JANET, 32

WHEN SHE PROPOSES

While chatting it up one night on the topic of women proposing,
the conversation quickly moved into the logistics of such a thing.
How would that work? Ellie chimed in, "Does she have a ring with
her when she proposes?" Sarah answered with her own question,
"Does that mean she buys her own?"

Just as there are many different wedding gown designers and
flower choices, there's not only one single way a woman (or a man,
for that matter) would, should, or could propose. There are no
rules. It does, however, boil down to three things—timing, honesty,
and results. But if you're planning on proposing, it might be a good
idea to consider three other things first—why, when, and how.

WHY

The most important thing to take into consideration is why you're proposing . . . and be honest and be yourself. There's a difference (no matter how subtle) in the whys and whats of proposing. If you're proposing because you're tired of him breaking into hives whenever you mention it, your motivation might be that you're fed up and not that you feel it's right. If you're just tired of him dragging his feet, you may want to hold off until you feel it's the right thing and the right time to propose, and not do it because you're ticked at him and want to eject yourself out of limbo.

Remember that women tend to feel ready for marriage before men do. Even if you think he may never be ready, proposing is not the answer right now if the mere mention of marriage is the sore spot in your relationship. His reactions to everyday engagement chats provide useful information as to where he stands on the subject. If he's clear to you that he's not ready yet to take this next step, proposing probably isn't the best step for you right now. However, talking to him about how you feel is.

If proposing seems right to you at this point in your relationship, and if your reasons feel emotionally backed by his actions and words, then go for it. If you can scream from the rooftops, "I'm going to propose because he's my best friend—my future husband. We have the most amazing relationship, and I feel it's the right step for us. And I know he feels the same"—then, girl, it sounds like you have reason to celebrate.

WHEN

Now it's time to move on to the second challenge to overcome. Timing. It's everything, so they say. Get a sense of whether the timing is in your favor (or if it's better to wait) with these simple questions. I know the point in proposing yourself is so you don't have to wait. But consider the following.

The timing might not be right if:

1. He's making subtle comments about marriage and how he's not sure it's for him. A few common phrases: ball and chain, not ready to settle down, his single friends have the life. You get the picture.
2. Tempers flared when you mentioned getting married this morning over eggs Benedict.
3. You spent your friend's wedding ceremony wiping your not-so-waterproof mascara off your cheeks. The kicker? They weren't tears of joy.

The stars are probably aligned if:

1. You feel you've both been enjoying your relationship for what it is—you're respectful of each other, you're best friends, and you're the perfect match.
2. You recently chatted about it, and you feel like you're both on the same page—wanting the same things out of marriage and the commitment that goes along with it.
3. You went to your friend's wedding last weekend and had a blast—not a struggle or fear in sight.

Factoring in the timing of the proposal can be the difference between your engagement being cause for celebration or cause for years of his lamenting about being pressured into things. If the timing just doesn't feel right, take that as subtle information about where your relationship is right now. If you want one thing and he wants another right now, it may not be smart to pop the question.

But this is still a great time to strengthen your relationship. Instead of asking, "Will you marry me?" you can ask to share more about how you each feel about getting engaged. This might be a good time to explore:

- What it is that you both want.
- What you want in your relationship that's not there now and what you need to do to get that.
- How you imagine things would be if you were married.
- How you see yourselves in two years.

Communicating your vision will give you the insight you need.

HOW

The third thing to consider is how your proposing will affect him. Will he feel cheated out of his manly right to ask for a woman's hand in marriage? Embarrassed? Disappointed? Or will he grab you in his arms, swing you around, and thank you for taking that pressure off of him?

I asked a group of men, "If your girlfriend proposed, would it affect your masculinity?" Responses varied, but most said it wouldn't affect their manhood. Some did say they'd feel like they missed their chance to really shine, and they'd be disappointed that they didn't get to propose. Others would find her taking charge sexy. And some are stuck in the old way of thinking that it's up to the guy to pop the question.

> It would throw me off. It's like the same visual that a little girl
> has about a big wedding. Well, I have a visual of proposing to
> somebody one day. And I want to keep that in my mind.
> Maybe that's old-fashioned. –CHARLIE, 33

I would have loved it; it would have taken the pressure off
me and been sexy in a nonconventional sort of way. But I'm
very happy with how things turned out with my proposing to
my wife. —DYLAN, 35

If you want to know how he'll respond, think back to any
signs he has given you about what proposing means to him. If
he's the romantic type who regularly surprises you with candlelit
dinners, bubble baths, and long-stemmed roses—then he may
be the type who would be bummed out that he didn't get to surprise you. If you're usually the planner, he may be relieved you
took the pressure off him. And if he gets turned on by you being
a woman who goes after what she wants—you'll be sure to knock
his socks off.

It wouldn't be the end of the world if she proposed. I would
have been happy. But as a guy, you see that as something
that a guy gets to do, as part of our culture, anyway.
You always wonder what it would be like the day you get
to do it. I may have been disappointed if I didn't get the
chance to propose. —SETH, 36

. . .

I wouldn't mind that she was the one to propose as long as
we talked seriously about getting married previously.
—MARTY, 33

. . .

I would feel like the decision was out of my control to some
extent, even though I had a yes/no say. It would feel like a
final decision about the relationship: If I say yes, we move on;
if I say no, it's over. I might be worried that the feelings and

readiness were one-sided—that's assuming I wasn't thinking
marriage at that point. —JIM, 38

SHE SAID "WILL YOU," HE SAID "I DO"

There are women out there who have bucked the system, got the
ball rolling with a proposal, and are now the proud wives of men
who said yes. When I found these hidden gems (so few and far between!), I asked one of them about her proposal story and what
made her decide to pop the question.

> My husband and I work in the same field, and we ended up
> meeting through friends at work. We were dating for three
> years when I proposed. I knew I'd found my best friend, my
> soul mate, and I just couldn't picture my life without him. We
> both knew we wanted to get married at some point. I
> proposed to him when we were away at a cozy little cabin in
> the mountains. When the moment was right, I asked him
> to close his eyes. Then I got down on one knee, and when
> he opened his eyes I was holding a box with his
> engagement/wedding band. I asked him to be my husband.
> He was absolutely speechless. He said, "I thought you didn't
> believe in proposing to a man?" I told him that he wasn't just
> any man, and that when you find your best friend, your soul
> mate—convention seems insignificant. I told him that I would
> love him and cherish him for the rest of our lives, that I
> would never hurt or deceive him, and that his heart was safe
> with me forever. He said yes! Proposing felt strange and a
> little frightening. This was really out of character for me—I
> was brought up to not even consider something like this. For

women thinking about proposing, it's important to be very sure it's something you both want. Don't propose just because you're tired of waiting for him to do it.

—LESLIE, 43

JUST THE TWO OF US

Here's a great question: How come when getting engaged is about two people, it's still assumed that it's up to one person (the man) to ask? I know the story goes back years and years, generations and generations, but what's stopping the woman from taking charge? Since marriage is teamwork, entering into it should be teamwork too. Why wouldn't two people decide together when to get married?

Notes from the Professor, Dr. Judye Hess

There should be discussion on why they can't decide together when to get married. Who says it's the guy that has to initiate this? Just like in sex. Does the guy always have to initiate? That would be a burden for the guy. Maybe it's time to abolish this notion that it has to be up to the guy to propose. Maybe that's outmoded. The guy asking the woman to get married comes out of asking her father for her hand in marriage. That's part of arranged marriages. Why are these people choosing to accept what society demands? They talk about feeling pressured from their family and society to do this, but they're buying into it. They're just saying that they have to play the game because that's the way it's played. Well, what if they choose to play it differently and just don't want to do this to themselves—and take control of their own lives?

I was out to dinner with family, and someone asked my husband's uncle, "How did you propose?" He said, "I didn't."

Some at the table were already familiar with the events that had transpired, but most of us gasped, "Huh?"

We intrigued listeners found out the story. The couple was dating for six years when they decided together they wanted to have children. They figured the first step to take would be to get married. They skipped the engagement and instead called up a rabbi they knew in the city and coordinated a date to meet at the rabbi's home to get married. They later celebrated their nuptials with a party. They literally skipped the "we just got engaged" and instead went right to "just married!"

Remember, it's not the ceremony and fanfare that makes a marriage—it's the union of two people. And boy, what a damper it would put on the wedding retail industry if word got out.

So what's needed to make more women feel comfortable about popping the question? After reading Malcolm Gladwell's *The Tipping Point*, I realized that what we might need to do is start a trend. Not one that involves hemlines or heel widths, but instead one that has women popping the question. Then more of us girls would feel empowered to follow suit.

Imagine if it became a popular thing, to be the one to take the bull by the horns (or your man by his collar) and just do it. Jewelry stores could tweak their ad copy a bit, changing "Thinking of proposing to her this February 14?" to "Thinking of proposing to him this Super Bowl Sunday?" What a trendsetter that would be!

FROM SUBLIMINAL TO SUBLIME

I was on the phone with my mother-in-law talking about how when a woman says he better ask or else, she didn't just propose. If anything, she's proposing he get the lead out. The conversation quickly moved into the truth behind the hints.

With all of this subliminal messaging going on, guys should know that things aren't always as they actually appear. (Tell that to the first guy who discovered she's wearing a Wonderbra!) But what's the point of our gestures, if we don't fill them in on their true meanings? So spread the word . . . the code is cracked! And here it is.

Action: A woman walks by a jewelry store and says, "Honey, let's go in for a quick browse—they may have the earrings I've been looking for." He's made it a few feet past the front door when she says, "Oh, and while we're here we might as well get my ring size. Since we're already here, of course."

Meaning: "If you're not going to get the ring rolling, then I am. Here's one check off your to-do list for moving this relationship forward. Now that you have my ring size, you can stop into any jewelry store and make your selection whenever the mood strikes."

Action: A woman keeps a mental note of all the times she is asked by friends, family, and colleagues if there will be a "Big Day" soon. Later on, she repeats all the comments verbatim to her guy: "Funny thing, Linda asked if our 'Big Day' is coming. Funny thing, Jess wants to know too . . ."

Meaning: "Do you see how often I'm bombarded? I'm your filter to all the other people who are asking the same question about when we're getting married. I'm one person bugging you, whereas I have countless people bugging me all day. We're both under pressure, so please try to understand my position."

Action: The No. 1 subliminal message of all: when a woman shares news of a friend's engagement. "Honey, guess who got engaged . . . Isn't that wonderful?"

Meaning: "I'm happy for our friends, but don't you think it's our turn now? We should be engaged too!"

News flash: Guys, when a woman announces a friend's upcoming nuptials, she's not just sharing good news. She's hinting for you to get off your butt and make a decision already. Of course, in her mind, the decision had better be to get engaged.

BREAKING THE MOLD

Something is stopping women from proposing. Instead they wait . . . and wait . . . and wait for their boyfriends to do it. And when a woman is playing the waiting game, no matter how crazy it's making her, why does she continue to play? I know it can be hard to break traditions, but isn't it time to stop the madness?

I asked one woman, "Would you ever propose to your boyfriend?" Without even thinking about it she firmly said, "No way." This quick response came from a woman who looked like she wouldn't wait around for anyone. Although in her office she was one to demand, "I want that business proposal on my desk by 3:00 P.M. or else," such a demand for another kind of proposal wasn't so easy to make at home. This came from a strict upbringing, something out of *Father Knows Best*. Chasing boys, to her family, wasn't proper. She wasn't allowed to even call them. Being so forward as to dial one of their numbers, well, that constituted a chase. She explained, "If I grew up not being allowed to phone a boy, how could I ever propose to one?"

If we learn of more and more women breaking old ways, perhaps more and more women will feel empowered to take control of the situation and pop the question instead of feeling as if they have to wait it out. Let's ditch Mom's old saying, "It's polite to wait to be asked." And if his answer isn't what you were looking for, it's better to find out sooner than later.

A tip from someone who's been there:

> Have a good idea as to whether or not they'd like to be proposed to and if they'd say yes. So hopefully you don't have any uncomfortable moments. I almost wish I'd brought it up before, so that we'd have had less conversation before he finally said yes. Decide in advance if he'd want a ring. Would he say, "Hey, if you're going to do it, I want it all, a ring, roses, the bended knee"? Or would that just be too much? I think once you ask, you shouldn't really expect a big engagement ring from him, as you took that option out of the equation. Always have a few good friends ready in case it all goes south. —MARGIE, 40

THE PROPOSAL—A HOW-TO

You've decided the timing is right, and you're ready to propose. That weight has been lifted, and now it's replaced with a bigger one: You decided to do this monumental thing . . . now how do you do it? Here are some tips to help you along.

When you picture your man proposing to you, would you ever say to him, "No, no, no. That's not the right way?" Of course not! So don't put unnecessary pressure on yourself to try to find the "right" way to propose. There isn't one. A proposal comes from the heart, so there's nothing wrong about it. But some things are helpful to think about beforehand—and will help you decide how to go for it.

First ask yourself how you see yourself proposing. When you start brainstorming on your own, you'll reflect on what represents the two of you. This way you'll be sure to come up with a proposal that's pretty spectacular—something that's so "you." Then it's important to determine if you're a planner or a go-with-the-flow girl. This makes all the difference in the world!

If you find yourself writing lists to organize your day, using Post-it notes to remind yourself to pick up your dry cleaning, and scheduling dinner with friends months ahead of time, then you might want to pop the question with plan in hand. You'll need to know the when, where, and how it will happen for it to go smoothly.

Be as creative as you want. Maybe you coordinate with the hostess at your regular Sunday night Chinese food restaurant to slip the words "Will you marry me?" into his fortune cookie. Or perhaps you print your proposal on the Frisbee you're tossing around in the park that sunny afternoon. When he catches it, he'll find out just what a great catch you think he is. Or perhaps you're more the type to do it up with candles, rose petals, and getting down on one knee. Take some time to brainstorm and jot down your own ideas on paper.

If you're the type who simply grabs the mike and says whatever comes to mind (prepared speeches are for wusses), then you might decide to pop the question organically. Perhaps it happens when you're on your nightly stroll through the neighborhood park and he accidentally steps in sticky bubble gum. Or one Sunday morning when you're in bed reading the paper and you realize how much you love him when he crinkles his nose at the sports scores. There's something to be said for when something so monumental is done naturally in a spur-of-the-moment flurry of excitement. The organic proposal is very similar to making a spontaneous toast—it comes straight from the heart. No props, no plans, just your genuine words—which are in themselves always complete.

WHICH IS BEST FOR YOU?

A plan in place: You decorate the walls with streamers and banners every year on his birthday. You even have an annual "Happy Valentine's Day" sign that goes up on the Day of Love. Planning for you is half the fun—you thrive on being creative and surprising him with special treats. You're the type that when you have to give a toast, you think it out well beforehand.

The spur-of-the-moment proposal: No decorated birthday cakes for you, and your motto is "no fluff." You're all about shooting straight from the heart, and you thrive best when you're not on a schedule. You do things when the timing just feels right.

RINGING THINGS IN

Since most proposals from men to women are accompanied by a diamond ring, you might be asking yourself how this will work if you're dropping to your knee. Historically the engagement ring is a symbol of the couple's commitment. Some women today see it as a status symbol, and others find comfort in it signifying being part of a couple. Take some time to learn what the ring means to you—so when you go to pop the question you'll have a sense of how you feel. Ask yourself if it's important to have a traditional diamond or if you're open to something different.

To put it bluntly, women who propose don't want to spend thousands on buying their own rings. It's sort of tough to picture, anyway—you propose to your beau, then slip a pear-shaped sparkler set in platinum . . . on your own hand. I just don't see that happening.

If you want to pop the question with some sort of ring, maybe consider proposing with matching engagement bands. From what I hear, most men don't love jewelry—but how about something simple like a thin silver band to mark the occasion? And if rings aren't your thing, yet you want to give him something special to celebrate your engagement—think of what's meaningful to you both. Just like with the proposal, sit down and really brainstorm. It could be something that he keeps with him (in his wallet or on his desk at work) to remind him of you and your engagement. Perhaps you write what you love about your relationship, what you love about him, or a list of your favorite moments together. A scrapbook filled with memories and photos. Something for his desk—like a photo of you two with lyrics to your song engraved. After all, it's the thought that counts!

If you don't want to miss out on the ooohs and aaahs that a hand with a sparkly diamond draws, consider choosing your engagement ring together after you propose. Or he may be attached to the idea of still surprising you with a ring. And, you never know, if you think alike he may even have something for you already. After guys make the purchase, they tend to hold on to the ring—sometimes for months even. Goes to show you truly never know what he's got planned.

AN UNEXPECTED RESPONSE

You have opened up your mind, heart, and mouth with a proposal. The room is silent, and your "Will you marry me?" is still floating through the air when your hopes are dashed with his answer—no.

Before you crawl under the nearest bed to cry yourself into oblivion, there's a way to get through this uncomfortable time, one moment that seems to last a lifetime.

Stay calm and clear up any misinterpretations immediately. Find out from your boyfriend what his response means. Is it "I actually don't see us getting married . . . ever?" Or does it mean "I'd love to get married one day, but I'm not ready for it right now"? Don't focus on your embarrassment, or how you should have listened to your sister who thought you were crazy. Instead, focus on his answer and explanation. These are the keys.

If the timing isn't right, take this time to explore together what it is that your relationship needs to take the next step. When you look back, you'll probably feel you both have grown from this relationship-discovery.

If you find out that you're writing two different scripts for your future, of course it will be difficult. But you know what you want—and you deserve to have it. If he's not on the same page, it's better to find out sooner rather than later, so you can open the door for "the right one" to come into your life.

BOUNCING BACK

Resilience specialist Dr. Beth Miller, a psychologist and author of *The Woman's Book of Resilience,* offers the following tips on how to stay strong if you don't get the yes you were hoping for when popping the question to your boyfriend.

- Make a list of your accomplishments/successes and nice things you have done for others. Keep the list visible.
- Remember what got you through rejections in the past. If you are still holding pain from previous rejections, do the

important inner work to transform the rejections into growth.

- Make this experience into an AFGO (Another F* Growth Opportunity).
- Buy yourself a pretty ring and vow to love, honor, and cherish yourself. [Wear it on your right hand!]

9

It's Your Thing—Do Whatcha Gotta Do

Sometimes women get so caught
up in the pressure to get engaged
that they don't consider if this
guy is good for them. Women
need to think about if their
boyfriend is someone who will be
there for them when they're sick.
Will he make a good father? Will
he make a good husband?
—HEATHER, 34

There might come a time in your relationship when you feel like you're waiting. Waiting for something. Anything. To happen. Something. It's almost the same feeling you get when you have an unexpected layover between flights, and you're stuck in the airport with nothing to do. So you wait. It's this relationship lull that causes the devil in Prada on your shoulder to start whispering, "Should I keep him or sweep him?" At the same time, you're fighting off the whispers in your other ear—your best friend's advice to start shooting out the ultimatums. (More on ultimatums in the next chapter.)

What's ironic is, this decision is very similar to his dilemma of whether to propose. Just like he's putting off the "for better or for worse," you're putting off the push for a change (for better or for worse). Instead of making the choice between enjoying your relationship for what it is or moving on, you uncomfortably wait . . . and wait . . . and wait. After all, if you ignore something, it will go away, right?

When I was going through my own case of the limbo, I'd phone the girls (and their husbands) to ask questions they couldn't possibly have the real answers to: "Do you think he'll propose?" "What is he waiting for?" And then there's the misery-loves-company approach: "Did you two go through this?"

Not only is it common for us to go over our story with whoever will listen, this verbalizing also gives us a chance to talk through and work out our plan of attack in our own mind: "Should I give him a deadline?" "Should I be nonchalant and act like I don't care?"

If you feel like your relationship is standing still (or even taking a few steps back), the more important question you owe yourself to dreadfully ask is "Should I stay or should I go?"

I was interviewed by a writer from a national wedding magazine on this very topic. In gathering information for her piece on why men stall when it comes to proposing, she asked me, "When do you tell a woman that enough is enough and it's time for her to move on?"

Even though there are red flags to determine if he's stringing you along, and signs to tell if his heart is in the right place, there isn't a universal formula. When and if to end it is an individual decision. Just like no one can tell you who you should fall in love with, and there are certainly no rule books for love, deciding on when you need to get moving is up to you. When you're stuck on when enough is enough, asking yourself the right questions can help you see the light on what's important and what can wait. Start off by uncovering a few of your feelings about the relationship overall and your commitment to each other. The first thing to uncover is what his plan is—is it a "we" or a "me"?

SIGNS THAT HE'S ON THE "WE" PLAN

Although he may not have proposed yet, your beau certainly does show signs that his aim is true and he's committed. For instance:

- Things are definitely moving forward (after all, you did just get a puppy together).
- He respects you and has let you know that he realizes that he can't take forever to get over his fears.
- You see that he's working hard to curb the jitters—he's even doing the work in counseling.
- He already bought airline tickets for you two to go visit his family next Thanksgiving.
- You know he wants marriage (with you)—it's just a matter of being ready at different times.
- Overall you have a fabulously healthy relationship—his not proposing is the only issue getting in the way of your enjoying it right now.

SIGNS THAT HE'S ON THE "ME" PLAN

There are certainly "thin ice" signs to watch out for. They're often more obvious than you think. It's just acknowledging that they're there, instead of skating right by them.

- Booty calls—he blows off your holiday office party but calls you to come over the same night at midnight.

- His brother's getting married and there's not an invitation for you in sight.
- He keeps talking about how you're going to get engaged, but five years have gone by and still no ring.
- He canceled your first scheduled wedding date—and not because the flowers he wanted for his boutonniere weren't in bloom that season.
- He's making plans to move to L.A., and the U-Haul he rented only has room for one person's things.
- He regularly makes promises he doesn't keep, no matter how small.
- You have more frustrated days in this relationship than happy ones, and it's not just because he's slow to pop the question.

Notes from the Professor, Dr. Judye Hess

There are people you meet who you just know have integrity. Then there are the fast talkers who can talk you into anything. If someone is giving you lines, and it sounds superficial, you need to figure out who you are dealing with. Talk is cheap. Anyone can say anything. Look at their actions.

Think about: Do they show up when you're in a stressful situation? Do they listen to you? Do they really seem to care? Will they give up their own needs to take care of you when you need them? Is this a person who's reliable? If they're not reliable with their family or other people, they won't be reliable with you either. Even if they are now, they won't be later, down the line.

KEEPING EYES ON THE PRIZE

One winter I saw this fantastic jacket online. I wanted it, wanted it, wanted it. Apparently I wasn't the only one, since they were on back order. I ordered it anyway, and kept checking to see when it would finally be delivered. Eventually, after what seemed like forever and a day, I finally got it. To my surprise, I realized that I didn't even really want it anymore. The season had passed, it wasn't that comfortable, and it didn't really fit my wardrobe. But while I was waiting for it to show up, I was convinced it was going to be the best thing ever.

Sometimes when we want something so badly, we forget why we wanted it in the first place. We get caught up in the "wanting" and the frustration behind the "why am I not getting," and we lose sight of whether what we originally wanted still fits in our life. This can go beyond new jobs and new styles and into old relationships. Women can get so caught up in the wanting to get engaged . . . they lose sight of the man they're wanting to get engaged to. It becomes a mission, a target, a mantra—get engaged . . . get engaged . . . get engaged.

There's also an investment factor to why most women wait out a relationship that seems to go at a snail's pace to the altar. Once a few years go by, women feel like they've already invested time in their relationship. It's like a project they've started—and why would they want to stop a project before it's finished? These women don't want to break up because they dread the idea of starting over. They think of all the time they have already put into this man. Given that marriage is one of the most important investments a woman will make—it had better be a good one.

People frequently ask, "What's the best age to get married?" In other words, what's the right age to commit to making this investment? There's no exact science to it. Like the stock market, we're always changing. The more experience you have, the better you know yourself, and the more grounded you are—all of these make strong building blocks for growing a relationship. I have heard women say that the guys they dated at twenty-two would never be someone they'd want to marry when they were thirty. Whereas some of my friend's parents met as young as fourteen, and they're still happily married. On the flip side, I also know couples that met when they were older, and they're already divorced. It depends on where you are in life when you meet your partner.

Many women are scared to start all over again. In many cases, I think they should. They'd be so much better off. But they feel, "Okay, I've committed this much, this amount of time, and there's no turning back." And they're willing to stick it out. Versus "You know what, this is the wrong guy. We're probably poorly suited for one another. He's probably not going to ask me. And it's this false hope." —EMILY, 31

YOUR MOST VALUABLE LISTENER

It started off innocently—a few laughs and shoulder shrugs when people asked you, "When are you two tying the knot?" But now you can no longer keep your cool. The clock has ticked its last tock. You're at your wit's end. Once you've hit this point of utter frustration, you start searching everywhere for answers. Your next-door neighbor. Your hairstylist. Even the UPS guy, if he'll stay long enough to listen. You're hoping someone can help you make the decision you know needs to be made. You want everyone's take on whether you should stay or go.

It's easy for friends and neighbors to shout out what they think you should do, because they don't have to actually do it. And there are obviously some times when their opinion is easy to take without a second thought—you look better in the pink sweater than the blue, you should take that new yoga class at the gym, the summer blockbuster you wanted to see is horrible. But, no matter how sound their advice is, with respect to the big stuff, you know it's up to you. So why not talk to someone you haven't really checked in with lately—yourself?

The thought of having an actual conversation with yourself might sound funny, but it'll help you get in touch with your take on the matter. You're the best person to check in with about how your relationship is going. Your answers will give you insight about what you really want without other people's influences.

When we start a conversation with someone else, we don't take notes. But when having a little self-exploration, it helps to have pen and paper handy. Jotting down your answers helps you think things out.

A LITTLE WORKOUT SESSION

When having "the chat" with yourself, these questions make good icebreakers:

1. What are my honest feelings about my relationship? How would I describe it?
2. How do I feel about myself in my relationship?
3. What do I want for the future of my relationship? What are my goals?
4. What has my boyfriend communicated to me that he wants from the relationship?
5. Do I see my relationship growing in the way I want it to?
6. What steps do I need to take to make my relationship feel the way I want?

MAKING THE LIST—IS HE NAUGHTY OR NICE?

Remember the days of writing out pro/con lists? They probably came in handy when deciding if you should move to New York or Los Angeles. Or when choosing between two different job offers. Well, here we go again. If you're stuck in the middle of deciding if you should stay or go, take out that pen and paper and list the pros and cons of each.

We all know that making (big) decisions can be overwhelming. And every decision we make has its good points and its bad. Just like when deciding to buy a house or accept a job, writing out what you like (and don't like) about each option allows you to take a step back. You're getting a good look at what you're deciding between. Seeing what's on your mind written down on paper helps bring clarity and helps you sort out your thoughts. And hopefully helps put an end to the spinning thoughts racing through your mind.

It might not be the easiest thing you've ever had to do, but at one point you have to take the steps to decide what's best for you. First, let's tackle if you were to stay in the relationship. That's sometimes the easiest. Make two columns on a piece of paper, labeling them PROS and CONS. What responses come to mind when you think about staying in your relationship? To get started, ask yourself a basic question. Does he make you smile during the tough times? That's a pro. Does he make your problems feel insignificant? Check in the con column. These questions are individual to each relationship, so only you can decide what needs to be asked.

This next one will be hard (considering moving on is always difficult). On a second sheet, list the pros and cons of moving on from your relationship. What comes up?

Don't be shy to consider whether you're choosing your relationship because your boyfriend is the man that you want to travel through life with, or because the idea of starting over and getting back into the dating scene seems like a drag. Be honest with yourself. Once you have these answers in a form that you can separate into the good, the bad, and the ugly, you can start to approach other aspects of the relationship.

THE TIMING OF THE SHREW— NOW OR NEVER

The common thread between women going through pre-engagement flux is their guys are dragging their feet. However, different situations play out. Some women hit that three-year dating mark and don't know where their relationship is headed. Some are figuring out if there's still a chance after he just postponed a previous wedding date. And others have no idea how their beau feels about marriage in the first place. How to get through this depends on the dynamic of the couple. Your timing depends on you.

When I was a guest on an online discussion forum, a man posted the question, "Why do women who want to get married hang on to relationships with men who don't want marriage?" It does kinda seem silly. If you want one thing, and he wants another, why be together? You wouldn't go dancing with someone who doesn't want to dance with you. Or take a vegetarian to a steak house. So if your man doesn't want to get married, why stay?

The reasoning is actually more complex than you think. It really varies depending on the context of why he doesn't want to get married. When he asked this question on why they stay, I responded with my own question: What exactly was he referring to when he wrote, "men who don't want marriage"? Was this in the context of an anti-groom? Was he referring to the guy who wants to get married one day but just not right now? Or was this about the guy who wants to get married but just not to his girlfriend?

Just as I wanted clarification on men who don't want to get married, women sometimes need an explanation from their man to find out where they stand. Does he want to get married, but just not now? Or is marriage not in the cards? Knowing this helps answer her own question of "to stay or not to stay." Before making a decision, it helps to have all the pieces of the puzzle. Only then can you see what's missing.

What helps women consider how to proceed with a relationship is having enough information from their beau. They need to know how he feels about getting married—the concept, the institution, the his and hers towels, the whole shebang.

It's helpful to be able to identify which description fits your boyfriend sooner rather than later. There's nothing like getting to the it's-getting-serious point, then you come to find out that nope, marriage is not in the picture for him. And as far as kids go, well, he'd be up for getting a puppy.

There are a few different reasons he could have for not wanting to tie the knot:

- He wants to get married . . . but not right now.
- Marriage is not for him . . . ever.
- He wants to get married . . . but for whatever reason doesn't see it happening with the two of you.

Words of wisdom haven't changed much over time. The age-old, time-tested advice for a happy marriage remains "Make sure you have the same values." For years we've been hearing that it's important to see eye to eye on money, marriage, and children. And with our hectic lives and busy jobs, what's new to the list is where you plan to live. So if his response is "I'm thinking of moving back east next year" when he sees you pick up Sunday's open house listings for West Coast homes—it might be the perfect time to check in.

HINTS IN A HURRY

Signs that let you know he wants to get engaged, but just not yet:

- The two of you have talks about your future—where you'll live, how many kids you'll have, where you'll retire.
- It's no secret; his feet are cold and no fuzzy slippers will warm them until he's ready.

- Aside from a ring on your left hand, he has placed everything he has in your relationship, and you feel he is fully committed to making it grow.

Signs that he's not marriage-minded:

- The words "I don't want to get married ever" have actually left his lips.
- He constantly puts down the concept of marriage, saying he doesn't understand why his friends who have "taken the plunge" gave up their freedom.
- He treasures his space and doesn't want to share it with you.

Signs it's not for the two of you (Who needs him, anyway!):

- When he talks about his future, he says things like "when I get married someday" or "when I have children," leading you to believe he isn't considering these things with you.
- You feel your relationship is moving backward. Instead of growing together, he's giving you signs that indicate he wants to grow apart, like not including you in family reunions or future weddings (and I don't mean yours).
- You can write out a laundry list of ways that show he's not committed to your relationship.

Although imagination can keep romance alive (what's in the box with the ribbon, where are we going to dinner for Valentine's Day, etc.), sometimes reality leaves a little less room for misunderstanding when it comes to the bigger things in life. This means having the scoop on issues that involve you (or don't involve you, in some cases):

- Does he want to move back to his hometown to be closer to his family?
- Is he planning on living out his dream of becoming a rock star?
- Will the shelves of your house be lined with photos of kids or with hockey trophies from his weekend league?
- And, for the big question, is he pro-marriage?

If you know his stance, you'll feel more in control. You'll feel in the loop. This way you can expend your energy that was previously spent wondering (and worrying) elsewhere.

In order for two people to move a relationship forward, you both need to have the same destination in mind. If you don't, you won't end up in the same place. I look at it this way: In order for a team to win a game, everyone on that team needs to work together to make it happen. I remember the words of my high school field hockey coach: "In order to win—everyone's got to want it." Just like with growing together and getting married—both people need to want it to make it happen. Couples are at their best and thrive when they feel like they're on the same team.

STRAIGHT FROM THE HORSE'S MOUTH

I was talking with Mandy about her boyfriend who was previously divorced. She was unsure if he ever wanted to get married again. I said, "Why not ask him?" The information isn't hidden in his PalmPilot or his sock drawer, so it has to come from him and can't be found during an afternoon snoop.

Once when I was researching something in a roundabout way, my brother said to me, "It's okay to go straight to the source and ask them what they know." It's just so simple that it's genius! And what a time-saver! The fast route is to ask the one who has the info—in this case, your beau. His stance will hopefully be pretty straightforward. That's unless he gives you one of those "I don't knows." If that's the case, how about asking him what he needs to do to find his answer?

So if it's not a given that marriage is in his future, discussing this with him should definitely be in yours. It won't be as comfortable as asking if he wants to go for a hike in the mountains or a jog in the park. But then again, it's not like you're asking if he'll meet you at the altar tomorrow. Being interested in hearing what he's looking for simply helps avoid any surprises later. Some women have shared with me that it wasn't until after three or four years of dating that they then found out that their boyfriend didn't want to get married—ever.

You obviously don't want to scare him into thinking you're planning your wedding for this upcoming Saturday, but being curious to learn if the agenda is getting married or not sounds reasonable to me. At the very least, it's good to know if you share the same vision and want the same things.

As we've already discovered, there are three basic groups of thought about proposing: the timing isn't right right now, the nervous Nellie, and the timing will never be right. Let's explore each of these situations and how they can shape your relationship and the decision on whether to keep it a couple.

WHEN IT'S JUST BAD TIMING

When Mitch and Rebecca met at a mutual friend's wedding, the chemistry was so obvious, everyone saw it. You could tell that Mitch was absolutely crazy about Rebecca and she thought he was a great guy. Although they had strong feelings, their lives were simply in different stages. She was turning thirty-two and looking for her husband, and he didn't want to think about marriage for another four or five years. Her idea of a fabulous Saturday night was throwing a dinner party, and his was getting the VIP table with friends at the new hot club downtown. Admitting to not wanting to give up the party life quite yet, he risked Rebecca not wanting to get involved. But he respected her and knew she deserved his honesty. From the beginning they were straight up about what they each wanted and realized a relationship wouldn't work. Rebecca opted out of starting a relationship with a man whose timing was off from hers. She knew she couldn't talk him into being on the same path she was on right now. And she didn't want to have to talk him into it either. So they decided to forgo the relationship for a strong friendship.

Even though they clicked right away, Rebecca and Mitch were both honest about what they wanted for right now. She was his (future) dream girl. She just showed up too early. He had some things to get out of his system, and he wasn't ready to meet her yet.

Flash ahead to what might have happened if they got involved. Their relationship probably would have headed in two different directions. She would have wanted something serious, and he would have been out for a good time. Communicating and seeing the signs from the beginning allowed them to avoid a game of tug-of-war. Neither wanted to start a relationship off with a whole lot of pushing and pulling.

WHEN IT'S A CASE OF THE JITTERS

If you're with the guy who wants to get married one day but is nervous about it, he's not alone. Although he probably feels like he is—think tumbleweed, a desert, a ghost town. That kind of alone.

But most men don't feel ready for that walk down the aisle in our time frame. This can be traced back to how girls would chase boys around the schoolyard, trying to catch a smooch from a less-than-interested young man. So how to deal with the beau who freaks out about marriage? The answer: Let him freak out.

The motto behind *His Cold Feet* could be "It's common for a guy to be both excited and nervous about getting married." But a guy may not be privy to this information. So the closer he's getting to actually proposing, the more nervous he gets. Which probably causes him to hold off on popping the question until the jitters pass.

So what makes these jitters disappear? The million-dollar answer is accepting them, realizing that it's okay to be excited and totally freaked out about something at the same time. Feelings don't have to be one way or another. And we have the capacity to have several different ones simultaneously. Haven't you ever heard of laughter through tears? We usually think, "I want to get engaged but am freaked out about it, so this must be a bad sign." It's not always easy to see that it's okay to feel a mix of emotions. Especially since men sometimes think in a more linear way—black or white, right or wrong, fixed or broken.

To bring it home for women what men are going through, let's look at what happens when we as women have to make a decision that only we can make but that involves our partner. I have friends who are dealing with their own "pre-pregnancy limbo." They want to start a family, and they want children (one day). But they're inundated with what-ifs: "What if the kids hate me when they hit middle school?" "What if I don't know what to do?" They have an image in their mind of how a mom-to-be should be and fear that they might not be maternal enough. They want to have kids, but at the same time they get freaked out about being responsible for a baby. So they buy more time. This is a glimpse of what the guys go through.

Waiting for him to realize it's just a case of the jitters can drive any woman crazy. While we're at it, our minds can play amazing tricks on us. He's not proposing because clearly his mother hates us. Or he's up late at night trying to patch things up with his ex. We've been known to think the worst at times. But underneath it all, there's really nothing like when we're in touch with our gut feeling. Sometimes it's just crystal clear, and when we have a good thing, we know it. So when he's going through the jitters, help him along with this quick and easy-to-remember plan:

J = Just relax
I = Involve yourself
T = Talk
T = Talk
E = Engage each other in your own personal fears about marriage
R = Really listen
S = Sit with what each other has said

Here are a couple of women who chose to stay put—looks like it comes down to good old female intuition.

I always knew he was thinking about us getting married, because he wanted to know what I would want for a ring. I drew a picture for him of what I would like, and he saved the paper and brought it to the jeweler. We knew we were going to get married; it was a matter of when. —HEATHER, 36

• • •

In general we have a great relationship. It's just this engagement stuff that's getting in the way.
—GAYLE, 33

WHEN MARRIAGE IS KNOT FOR HIM

If you have to ask, "Does he want to get married ever?" your man is probably one of two types: the been-there-done-that divorcé or the confirmed bachelor. Sometimes going through a divorce just once is enough to make him not want to tie the knot. Or maybe it's because he already has children and thinks, "Why get married again?" If he's a confirmed bachelor, he might be stuck in the fantasy of the James Bond approach to lovin'—quantity is better than quality.

Got yourself an anti-groom? If you know this off the bat, ask yourself why you're holding on to someone who doesn't want the same things. Do you think he'll change his mind? You'll be the one to tame the wild beast, or maybe show him that marriage is worth a second try. Sure, anything's possible. But don't hold your breath.

Instead of holding on to the hope that he'll propose one day, stop waiting around and consider how his not wanting to walk down the aisle affects you. Ask yourself, "Can I live with that?" Would you be okay continuing in this relationship without one day writing out place cards, fluffing a veil, and signing on the dotted line? Or does that marriage certificate mean too much to you to give it up? Think about it. If you go against what you really want, that in itself will get in the way of your happiness. You'll always feel like you gave something up, and you'll resent him for it later.

Joan was dating her boyfriend for a little over a year when she found out that he didn't want to get married again. He went through a rough divorce, and getting married just didn't appeal to him. She felt blindsided when she learned that he too wasn't thinking up the details of an intimate second wedding. I asked her if they'd ever talked about this before. She said, "Well, sort of. He has told me that he wouldn't get married again, but I didn't think he really meant it. After all, we just moved in together."

If you're dating a guy who says he doesn't want to get married, believe him. He's being honest with you, so you should be honest with yourself. You should also know that his decision probably has nothing to do with you. All of your insecurities may creep up, and before you know it you're thinking, "If only I was good enough, then he would get married again and marry me." When this starts to happen, picture your best friend saying, "Hold it right there!" and stop putting yourself down. She's right, his stuff has nothing to do with you.

Take my friend's dad, for instance. His first marriage left him a widow, and his second marriage left him in divorce court. The only thing he experiences when he thinks of reply cards, table numbers, and a cake cutting is cold sweats. It wouldn't matter which supermodel walked through his front door—for him, the third time is not a charm. This is an issue that has absolutely nothing to do with his current girlfriend. It has everything to do with his past experiences.

So what do you do if you really love this person who doesn't want to get married again? Do you settle? No, you don't have to. He's made his decision. Now you have to make yours. Will what he wants work for you? After all, he's told you that what you want doesn't work for him.

I recently met a woman who lives with her boyfriend. They each have a child from a previous marriage, and they're both happy with their relationship the way it is. She told me that she doesn't need that legal paper tucked away in a drawer somewhere. And she meant it.

She's always dodging questions from other women waiting for their boyfriends to pop the question. They ask, "How could you not want to get married?" Don't get me wrong, she's not an anti-bride. She enjoys weddings—as long as they aren't hers.

Her beau isn't completely off the hook. After we talked for a while, I learned that she may not need the wedding, but she does want the ring. Not necessarily a two-carat sparkler, but something to symbolize their commitment. Since neither one of them feels the itch to get married, this arrangement works for them. Just like two people have to want to get married to make it happen, two people need to not want to tie the knot to be happy.

10

Keep Him or Sweep Him
and the Scoop on Ultimatums

I have a [biological] time clock
and it's ticking.
—STEPHANIE, 28

Maybe it's your clock ticking. Maybe you would rather not have your gray hair competing with your white veil. Or it could be all the bridal showers you've been enduring lately. (One more wedding dress out of tissue paper and you'll scream!) Whatever the reason, something makes us give the guy dragging his feet a little push to get him going. But if you're dating a guy who says he doesn't want to get married, this is when you need to give *yourself* a little push to call the shots. Don't just go with the flow and let years slip by. Bitterness and resentment are the only things at the end of that rainbow.

When you're with a bachelor-wannabe, it's really up to you to decide if you want to stay with a man who doesn't want the same things. Will you be happy in your relationship without the Mr. and Mrs.? If you've decided that a piece of paper from a court or church won't make or break your relationship, can you feel secure in this relationship anyway? When two people want different things, it comes down to just that—you want different things. You can still make it work, if you both respect these differences and move forward with them in mind.

If a guy told you he didn't want to get married, it's tough not to take it personally. Feelings of rejection start stirring. Is it because he's buying more time or because he's anti-wedding? Is it you or the institution? Instead of wondering about him, ask yourself if you really want to be with a man who doesn't want what you want. Once you start calling the shots and asking the questions, you'll feel more empowered. Now you can start making decisions based on what you want. Keeping the ball in your court will even give you enough confidence to move on, if the need arises.

FAQ

Question: I've been with my boyfriend for three years. I know I want to get married one day, and he's not sure. How do you know when it's time to move on?

Answer: The big question is whether you feel it's time to move on. If you're at the place of deciding whether you should stay in your relationship or not, several things are very important. Have you shared completely with him how you feel? Do you have information from him on where he stands on marriage? Have you two talked about what it is that he's not sure about? Do his fears have to do with marriage itself, or are there issues in your relationship that make him hesitant? Listen carefully to his answers and compare them to what you feel in this relationship. Do you believe he's being honest with you? Knowing what you want will tell you if it's time to move on.

Question: My boyfriend of four years just told me that he doesn't want to get married and he doesn't want kids. I think it's because his parents went through an awful divorce—the whole idea of marriage shakes him up. I've always wanted to get married, and I'm not sure what to do. We have a fabulous relationship, and I can't imagine leaving him over a big white dress. Can I move forward with this new info?

Answer: Take time to really (and I mean really) think about how you would feel about not having kids and about not getting married. Is this a deal breaker for you? Find this answer. Don't move forward hoping you're going to change his mind.

KEEPING HIM: THE POWER OF A TIME FRAME

If you decide to stay in your relationship, it's important to manage the stage that you're in rather than let the limbo take over your life. When marriage is something you want, it's important to talk to him and to yourself. In the conversation with him, share your feelings—although you love him, you want marriage, and you need to set a time limit as to how long you can wait for him. In the chat with yourself, set that time frame.

You're giving him a gentle but firm time frame that you've set for yourself, not an ultimatum that you've set for him. This is where things can get fuzzy. Isn't a time frame an ultimatum? Here's the difference:

An ultimatum is telling him that if he doesn't do something by a certain date, then he's out of the picture. It might sound something like this: "If you don't propose to me by my birthday, I'm outta here." An ultimatum will only push his buttons. His pride and stubbornness will get in the way. (No one tells him what to do.) Then he'll feel more pressured, which may mean he'll back off even more. It's a no-win situation, so avoid it.

However, a time frame is much more approachable. It's not a push. It's a gentle nudge that might sound like this: "I love you, but at the same time I know that having a marriage commitment is important to me. I really need to set a time frame for myself as to how much longer I can stay in this relationship without that. If I choose to keep going on without a commitment, I know I will only grow resentful . . ."

You're being honest. You can't wait forever. You've used "I statements" to express how you feel and to remind him that marriage is important in your book. You haven't set demands on him, but only on yourself. Instead of continuing to wonder what's taking him so long, you're reminding yourself how long you're willing to wait.

Make a parallel with another common life decision. You get a job offer from company #1. The employer needs to get the show on the road but gives you a fair amount of time to decide if you're on board. If they don't hear back from you, they check in. If you're still not sure, needing to move forward, they thank you kindly but then move on to the next candidate. That's business.

Now, picture you get a job offer from company #2. They demand an answer by 2:00 P.M. on Friday or else that's it. That sort of demand just raises your blood pressure. Can't exactly see yourself in that kind of a pressure-cooker environment for the rest of your career, right?

Even though company #1 may be trying to achieve the same thing (your yes or no decision), they let you know in a fair and reasonable way. Instead of feeling a demand has been put on you, you feel that, although they're excited for you to join their team, they really can't wait forever to hear back from you. It's all in the art of the communication.

Still don't see the difference? You may think that giving your own time frame just sounds like a sugarcoated ultimatum, a little wishy-washy. Not so. Even though you're getting the same point across that you're not waiting forever, it's how you say it that makes all the difference. It's in the tone. When I hear, "If you don't propose to me by my birthday, then I'm leaving," right away I think ultimatum. And it's a high-pressure one. Bad move. When I hear, "While I understand that you're not ready, I do want to marry you, but at the same time I have my limits as to how long I can wait . . . ," I hear a woman letting her boyfriend know how she feels and that she has a time frame for herself. Pressure he feels from that would be self-imposed.

MORE ON ULTIMATUMS

Shit or get off the pot. Fish or cut bait. Colorful catchphrases that your sister, best friend, and coworker are telling you to tell him. Seems they all think these lovely demands are the answer to getting your beau to propose. Then there's the popular "Leave and he'll come running" or "He's not proposing because he's comfortable, so make him uncomfortable." And then the doozy—give him an ultimatum.

You want to put an end to his broken record, "We'll get engaged soon." Especially since the "soon" he spoke of was said two years ago. The limbo's gone on too long, and as you're rethinking strategy you start to wonder, "Will giving him an ultimatum do the trick?"

What do you think of when you hear the word "ultimatum"? For me, images of threats and demands immediately come to my mind. And when I Googled "ultimatum," that's exactly what came up: The word is used when two countries are battling and no more negotiations are on the horizon. One country gives the other an offer to accept or reject. If what's put on the table is not accepted, they go to war. There's no talking about it.

I asked a group of people to tell me the first thing that comes to mind when they hear "ultimatum" and to give an example of what one would sound like. Here are some responses.

If you don't do something, then you suffer some unfavorable consequence, like "If you don't propose by this date, that's it!" I wouldn't respond favorably to an ultimatum. If someone isn't sure if they're ready to commit, then giving an ultimatum may make them do something their heart is not really in.

—JODI, 35

• • •

I hear ultimatum and I think, "I'm not doing it!" —ROB, 35

• • •

An ultimatum, to me, is one last chance. It only works if the person delivering the ultimatum has a record of being strong and following through on past promises. If it comes across as just another idle threat, it lacks credibility and will likely not work. —BECKY, 52

• • •

The word "ultimatum" really is a big turnoff. However, it's really important for a person in a relationship to be clear on

what he/she needs and to make decisions based on where
one wants life to go. You can't wait forever! –RAYNA, 33

Ultimatum gone wrong: "We better be engaged by my birthday
or else!" Why it goes wrong? It's a threat—something people don't
generally respond well to. This isn't third grade, and you're not
threatening the playground bully to back off or you'll get your big
bro's buddies to kick his/her butt. This is a demand that will affect
someone you love. Underneath it all, there will be resentment.

Ultimatum gone right: "Although I love you, I do want marriage in my life and can't wait forever to find out if we're on the
same page." Why this goes right? You're letting him know how you
feel, and you'll feel empowered doing so.

As I was writing *His Cold Feet*, I found that the meaning of an
ultimatum is up for interpretation. Some thought they gave their
boyfriends an ultimatum just by telling them they wanted to get
engaged. Others agreed with me—it's a demand, and not a place
they were interested in going.

There are two types of ultimatums: the hard sell and the soft
shoe. Let's look at the differences.

A hard ultimatum is setting a demand with a consequence.
Take a look at Merriam-Webster's online dictionary's definition of
ultimatum: a final proposition, condition, or demand; *especially*
one whose rejection will end negotiations and cause a resort to
force or other direct action.

As kids, these hard ultimatums were dished out to us all the
time. From moms who say, "If you don't eat your broccoli, then
you get no dessert." From teachers: "If you talk out loud one more
time, then no recess." These no-fun ultimatums only make kids
cry, leaving them without a clue as to why they're supposed to eat
their broccoli in the first place. If the reasoning behind the veggies

was explained (they're good for you), they would get it. It may not make them eat the greens on their plate, but at least they'd understand why they weren't getting ice cream.

Now let's take a look at a soft ultimatum. This is letting someone know where you stand by sharing your feelings and your experience. And in terms of limbo, it's getting your point across that you're not going to wait forever for him to make up his mind.

The hard ultimatum given to him: "If you don't propose by New Year's, then that's it!"

The soft ultimatum (also known as the ultimatum you've given yourself): "I want to let you know that I love you and I would love for us to get married." (Fill in the blank with why you want the commitment and give examples whether it has to do with wanting kids, a family, a committed relationship, etc.) "But I have my own time frame. I'm letting you know that at some point, if we're not engaged, I'm going to have to move on."

It's a lot longer, but it's way more powerful. At this point, you set a time frame for yourself. And it's just for you. If you think you might have trouble sticking to it (which is the most important part), tell your closest friend. She'll keep you in line. If he doesn't propose within whatever time frame you have, then you move on. The thing to remember is that the point is not to manipulate him into doing (or not doing) something. It's to explain your feelings so he understands you. Then he'll make his own decision as to what he wants to do. Then you act accordingly. Do what you wanna do.

If you give someone an ultimatum and they feel pressure to get married, that's going to be an issue in the relationship. The goal isn't to be married. The goal is for two people to want to marry each other. If you're honest with him, then he'll get to a place where he wants to get married,

as opposed to feeling like he has
to get married. —DAVE, 38

If he understands where you're coming from, he'll respect you and make a decision one way or the other. Besides, when a guy feels like he's being told what to do, chances are he's not going to want to do it. No matter what it is. Fix it or else. Buy it or else. Marry me or else. Ultimatums backfire when he feels like you're bossing him around, something he already fears will happen once you tie the knot. Throw a demand in his face and his fears are now a reality. Get ready to watch him run faster than the Road Runner.

PUTTING TIME ON THE TABLE

You want to let him know you mean business. You're as desperate as a Hail Mary pass. You're not waiting around forever. So say it in a way that doesn't sound like a demand. There are two straightforward steps:

1. **Let him know you've made a decision for yourself— you're not comfortable in continuing this relationship without a commitment.** If you're honest about how you feel, then he shouldn't feel pressure. You aren't telling him he needs to do something by such-and-such a date. You're just letting him know where you stand. And with that information he can choose the direction that he wants to move.
2. **Mean what you say.** Women agree on this cardinal rule. If you choose a soft delivery when making your semi-ultimatum instead of a demand, it doesn't mean you

should be soft in sticking with it. In fact, if you stay with instead of sway from your decision, he'll be more apt to take you seriously.

VARIOUS WAYS OF WORKING WITH THE ULTIMATUM

Here is what a few women had to say on ultimatums and their own experiences with (and without) them.

Telling this is embarrassing, considering some of the romantic and thoughtful things some men do, but Larry has been the very best husband possible for thirty years!

We were dating for a year, and Larry was eight years older than me. My mother . . . told me to forget Larry . . . He was thirty-two, and she said he would never settle down. I was without a doubt wasting my precious years, in her opinion.

So I did all the game playing. My roommates and I would leave messages to each other so that our now husbands would see that other guys had called. My roommate Betsy even stooped to sending herself flowers from a fictional man. I told Larry I wanted more and started dating. Then I told him I wanted a diamond, and he got me a diamond necklace. "Not quite what I had in mind!" I told the poor floundering soul. Whatever it was, he decided to tie the knot! In my heart I don't think it's as exciting with the ultimatum—I'd love the surprise and romance, but the years were ticking by and pressure from everywhere was telling me to get to the next phase of my life. —ELLA, 55

I did indeed give my husband an ultimatum to get married. He was very young, and we had only been together eighteen months, but he had moved to New York City from Beantown after college and just assumed I would follow. Little did he know that I had had many a conversation with the "terminal girlfriends" who warned me to never move without a diamond on your hand and a deposit on the hall. They neglected to follow their own advice and were living in limbo hell. I confirmed this with the closers (I mean wives) who said they heeded this advice and had all relied on the power of ultimatums, sometimes referred to by men as bribery. Oh well . . . it works! –LAUREN, 42

• • •

Interestingly, I didn't give an ultimatum. I realized Jared and I were at the point where I would need to, in order to move forward, but that's not my style. So I ended it. Because how good a marriage would it have been if I had given an ultimatum? Not good, so I punted. –SUZY, 32

• • •

I had this realization that my girlfriend was willing to wait for me—she wasn't giving me an ultimatum. She would say, "I want to be married," and she was honest with her feelings. That was different than an ultimatum. This wasn't nagging at all. –RYAN, 34

THE UNIQUE ULTIMATUM

I know a woman whose boyfriend wanted to move from New York to San Francisco for a job. He wanted her to make the coastal jump with him. Understandably, there was no way she was picking up and moving cross-country without a ring on her finger. And she told him so: "I'm not moving to San Francisco unless we're engaged." She explained to him where she was coming from: "I can't pick up and uproot my life without a commitment." When a guy hears a concrete reason for something, he understands better. In this case, her boyfriend understood why she didn't want to pick up and move without being engaged. Leave out your reason, like a mom telling her kids no dessert, and guys don't think of where you're coming from. All they see is how they're being pressured and told what to do.

SWEEPING HIM

If the timetable talk didn't go the way you anticipated, there's a right reason to sweep him and a wrong reason to sweep him. Sweeping him to get him to propose is the wrong reason. Yes, he may come running. But then again, he may not. A right reason to sweep him is because you can't seem to see eye to eye on marriage.

BOUNCING BACK

Resilience specialist Dr. Beth Miller offers a few more tips on how to bounce back after a breakup and how to get through the transition from ending a long-term relationship.

On calling it quits:

- Have an "I quit" party, with everyone you love and who loves you. The price of admission is to be ready and willing to tell a personal story of quitting.
- Make a list of all the freedoms and gains you get from being on your own. (Get friends to help.)
- Catch up on movies, books, and friends you haven't had time for.

- Have a good cry in the shower and/or on someone's shoulder.

On bouncing back from a breakup:

- Make a scrapbook or collage of your strengths/talents/gifts. Keep it visible.
- Do something nice for someone else.
- Make use of the freedom—a time you don't have to make a partner happy or see to his needs or compromise. Enjoy leaving the top off the toothpaste, having popcorn for dinner, cleaning (or not cleaning) to your heart's content.

If it's a clean break, it will be difficult at first—as separation always is. Line up support for yourself, even before the damage is done. Although you decided to end the relationship, it doesn't make the break any easier. Loneliness is going to kick in since you're used to spending so much time with him. Not a bad time to lean on your friends. They'll understand. And sure, watching *Sex and the City* marathon reruns and renting John Hughes movies all weekend makes any girl feel better, but staying busy and doing nice things for yourself will keep your spirits up.

If you were going to do something nice for yourself, what would you do? Some ideas from those who've been there:

- Treat yourself to a mani and pedi at the best salon in town.
- Train for a road race to benefit a nonprofit organization that you love.
- Take up yoga.

- Join a gym. (Getting those endorphins going is proven to help fight the blues.)
- Plan a Girls' Night Out—no boys allowed.
- Start to read a fabulous new book.
- Visit a close friend for the weekend.
- Take a dance class.
- Learn to cook. (Nourishment is always good.)

Most of all, stay curious. Remember, when one door closes, another one opens. Of course it's too soon to consider dating again (you have a lot of healing to do), but you should always keep your lessons in life in the back of your mind as you move forward. If marriage is in your plans and the day comes when you find yourself on a date with a gentleman who has potential to be your new beau, why not find out early on if it is in his too? This is obviously *not* first-date conversation, but it's important to discover these things about each other. It's not like you're suggesting he propose tomorrow. Today, you're just finding out if you want the same things.

During a breakup, it's common to kick back on the sofa with a pint of Häagen-Dazs to ponder what he's thinking. Does he miss you? Will he come around? The questions are endless, and so is the tub of ice cream. You might even "accidentally" run into his best friend to find out. But instead of wondering what he thinks— take this time to consider what you think. How do you feel about this guy who couldn't make the commitment you wanted? Don't worry about how you're being judged by him. It's your time to do the judging.

MOVING OUT—DON'T MAKE IT A GAME

I asked people what advice they would give to a close friend who wanted to get engaged to a guy who wasn't ready yet. Responses had a common thread across the board. If the couple I asked about was living together, they advised, "She should move out." The hope is that if he loves her and wants to get married, then he'll follow after her, ring in hand.

Sometimes the saying "You don't know what you have until it's gone" rings (no pun intended) true. And yes, it happens. She moves out with a graceful stoic exit, and he turns to mush. His phone calls start. "I love you. I miss you. You're the one for me."

I consider this a game. I love games. Ones with dice. Or cards. Scrabble and Boggle. But ones like this . . . I'm not a fan. I don't believe in doing something just because you're trying to get someone to respond a certain way. More often than not, she moves out and instead of a new response of love from her man, she ends up with a new lease, new boxes that need unpacking, and the new decision as to where she should put her ficus plant.

The only time I think packing the bags is a good idea is if a woman will be okay if he doesn't come a-chasing. The next knock on her door might just be the pizza guy. Moving out because you think it will get him to propose and moving out because you really believe it's the right thing to do are two totally separate issues. One's a game. One is in your best interest.

ON TAKING HIM BACK

It's an age-old story. Guy breaks up with girl. It's tough at first, but she deals. She might have even joined an online dating service and posted a profile. So she's out and about. She's meeting new people. She's filled up her weeknights with everything from cooking classes to yoga classes. This is where the "he" comes back into the picture. He calls. He wants to get together. With her busy schedule, it's not so easy to fit him in for dinner and a movie. This is when "he" turns into "blubbery he," telling her, "I miss you. I want us to get back together. Life is so hard without you."

This is when she asks, "What should I do? Do I take him back? How do I know if he'll pull this again or not?"

This is where I come in to ask, "Well, what do you want to do? Do you want to take him back?" And the one everyone loves: "What would make you want to take him back?"

Again, there's no concrete formula to determine whether a woman should take back a boyfriend who previously broke her heart. Nor is there a way to forecast if he will pull the same shenanigans again or not. But there are some things to consider that can give you information to help you answer your question.

You can learn a lot about a person by how he did the breaking up. That in itself is valuable information about a person's character. A guy who ends it ranting and raving because you were pressuring him to get married is very different from the guy who expresses that it seems like you're in two different places right now.

Want to know who you're really dealing with? Here's a little quiz to help give you a look:

QUIZ

1. Did you find out from his best man that he (and I don't mean the best man) wouldn't be showing up for your Big Day?
- a. That's exactly what happened!
- b. No. He'd never do that. He was very communicative all along about his hesitation.

2. Did you come home one day and much to your surprise find a moving truck in your driveway?
- a. That's exactly what happened!
- b. Nope, would never happen. We talked about how we'd be there for each other through this transition.

3. You saw the breakup coming. He had been expressing his feelings all along.
- a. Are you kidding? This breakup was completely out of the blue!
- b. Yes, we both tried to give it our best to make it work for quite a while.

Picked A's? Would you dare let your best friend take this guy back if this was her issue? Probably not! Picked B's? Sounds like a pretty amiable break. If you feel that his heart was in a good place—decide how you would feel trusting him with your heart again. Does it feel safe?

When considering if you should give him a second chance, think about how he supported you after the breakup. Did he ask you to never phone again, or did he call you to check in to see how you were doing?

If he left you at the altar . . . well, I don't know about you, but

I'd have a hard time standing a friend up if we had plans to meet at a movie.

GETTING BACK YOUR POWER

Beyond the proposal, timetables, and calendar pages, the bottom line is always going to be how you feel in the relationship. Don't be afraid to ask yourself powerful questions. How do you feel treated? How do you feel about yourself in this relationship? You deserve nothing but the best, and you want someone who supports this.

Instead of getting wrapped up in worrying about when he's going to propose and why it's not now, figure out how you feel. Putting too much thought into what he thinks and not enough into what you think takes away your power. Don't worry about how you're being evaluated. ("Does he want to marry me?") Do some evaluating yourself. Decide what you want and how that can be accomplished. That in itself will bring you back to feeling empowered and like that confident woman that you are.

If you're having trouble getting in touch with how you feel and what you want, a good therapist, coach, or counselor can help you navigate the process. Getting to know your answers to important questions is a valuable experience.

FINDING A THERAPIST

To find a good counselor, therapist, or coach, ask a trusted source like your doctor or a friend for a referral. The American Psychological Association provides referrals for therapists: www .helping.apa.org. The International Coach Federation has a coach referral resource on its site, "Find a Credentialed Coach":

www.coachfederation.org. The National Board for Certified Counselors has "Find a Counselor" on its site: www.nbcc.org.

Questions to ask a coach, counselor, or therapist:

- Do you provide a complimentary consultation? (It may take a little searching before finding someone you feel comfortable with.)
- What are your credentials? (Ask about licensure, certification, and experience.)
- What type of training do you have? (If you're curious about where someone did his/her training, feel free to ask.)
- Do you have a specialty? (It's helpful to know if your coach or therapist specializes in a particular area. If you want to talk about your relationship, picking a career coach probably wouldn't work for you.)

Quite frankly, the best way to find out where you stand is to tell the guy how you feel. Let him know that you're going to have to make some choices and do what's best for you. Give the guy six months to do something. If he doesn't do it, then it's time to go. —JACK, 30

Notes from the Professor, Dr. Judye Hess

I think she has to know whether or not this guy is going to be someone who is never going to commit. She might be picking up on something, if she's feeling continually abandoned. He might be telling her, "Don't worry, we'll get married someday." But there are people out there who will never, when the chips are down, get married. And it's important to identify when you are involved with one of them. Especially these days, people are living together. Men have the house, they have the security, they have the sex—they don't care about the ring. So how do we know when this person is a bad risk? Some signs to look for are:

- Does he promise things, then not deliver?
- Is he continually late to meet you—and makes excuses that it wasn't his fault?
- Is this person generally untrustworthy and unreliable?

It's not just one area. You need to look to see if someone can't make or keep a commitment in all sorts of situations, and how much responsibility he takes for his own behavior.

If a woman doesn't know if this guy is for real or not, I would recommend doing some couples therapy. Because the woman in the relationship wants so much for this guy to be the right one—she might not be that objective. A third person [a therapist] can often see the dynamic in a few sessions.

Whether or not there's a time frame to hold out would be case specific. In the 1950s musical Guys and Dolls, Nathan and Adelaide were engaged for fourteen years. Adelaide sings this song about a woman developing psychosomatic symptoms while waiting for this marriage to happen. This was back in the '50s—this issue has been going on for a long time.

There are two things to remember: (1) Build up your own self so you're not so dependent on the relationship for self-esteem, and (2) check in with someone else if it feels like it's going on too long. Too long may be dependent on what your goals are. Maybe your biological clock is running out and you feel you need to get on with it. Or maybe you just reached your level where you're ready for a commitment. And if it *looks like this person isn't going to go through with it, then you want to check in with yourself about your needs.*

WHATEVER YOUR DECISION, IT'S YOURS

If you decided to keep him, try to enjoy your relationship the way it is right now. Give yourself a break from all of the engagement pressure and try to just "be" in your relationship. If you find yourself stuck in a rut, remember that you have the choice and the control to decide in which direction you want to navigate.

Once you've decided that your happily-ever-after doesn't come stapled to a marriage license, you're still probably going to want to signify your (nonmarital) commitment. Take some time to talk about how you each define your partnership. And decide together on what you can do to mark the occasion. Maybe you want to plan a weekend away to reminisce about your years together and your vision for the years to come. If you want to celebrate your relationship with those you love (and if you always wanted the party), throw a party. You can even write your own vows to each other. Having something that's special and between the two of you will help solidify your relationship. For better or for worse.

Decided to sweep him? I know it will be difficult at first. But, as I would say to a friend who is going through a breakup, "I'm sorry you have to go through this. And at the same time, I'm excited to see what's next for you." You now have the chance to let someone in who's wonderful for you. Stay curious. Can't wait for you to meet him!

11

Your Happily-Ever-After: A Final Wrap-up on Pre-engagement Limbo

It's important to have the same
picture for what makes a
happy life.
—TRACEY, 34

When one woman finds out another made it through pre-engagement limbo, it's a free-for-all. The notepads come out. The cell phone is put on vibrate. All ears are open. The unengaged becomes uninhibited and descends upon her successfully engaged counterpart like she's the new spring line of Louis Vuitton bags. The first question she asks is "How did you get him to propose?" That is followed by "What did you do?" and "What was your strategy?"

Everyone's looking for the secret ingredients in getting him to ask, "Will you marry me?" But as we've learned, it's not about gaining some secret strategy.

You can get him into the habit of putting the toilet seat down or putting his dirty clothes in the hamper. But the truth is, no woman really wants to hypnotize her guy (you will propose, you will propose) or wave a magic wand over his head to get him down on one knee. Why? Because, although it might seem appealing, deep down inside there's an element that would be missing if you controlled the reins—the element of surprise.

Even though women want to know how to make it happen, they want him to want it to happen. Besides, if this were a fairy-land tale, any pop-the-question potion would eventually wear off anyway. Then you're left with something worse than your prince turning into a frog—he would become a moping husband, down in the dumps because he feels like you forced him into doing something he wasn't ready for. Every problem in your relationship might boil down to "Oh yeah? Well, you made me get married before I was ready."

Even worse, when a guy feels bullied into doing something, from that point forward you will have lost all negotiating power for any matter to follow. Why? Because it hurts his pride thinking he gave in to being told what to do. Which might enhance his stubborn edge.

YOU'RE NOT THE BOSS OF HIM

Guys fear that once they're married, they won't have a say in how things go. Leading up to that day, they want to make sure their voice is heard, especially when it comes to big decisions. Wouldn't anyone? For instance, I know a couple who has been married for a few years. Both want kids. That was never an issue. For as long as I can remember, he was ready, and she was totally freaked out by babies. She was pretty hard on herself: "Before becoming a mom, I should be more responsible. I still don't pay my bills on time. I haven't been to the dentist in a year." It wasn't until she took some advice from a dear friend that she felt ready: "You don't have to have it all figured out. You'll learn as you go. Besides, if you're not ready now, you'll never be ready. But if you know you want to have a family—you should go for it. You'll be a great mom!" Once these words sank in, it was a huge relief. Now she was ready. Just when you'd think she and her husband were on the same page—not so fast. She got so excited about this new phase, it was all she could talk about to her hubby.

"I'm so excited to have a baby!"
"I like these names for a girl . . . and these for a boy . . ."
"We need to start looking at bigger houses."
"When we have kids, we should get the Volvo."
"Do you think your mom would come out here to help?"
"We should probably start asking around about a nanny."

She had the color picked out for a Bugaboo, and she wasn't even preggo yet.

The hubby who wanted kids had now started to freak out. Was it pressure? Did he feel overwhelmed? A big house, a new car, a nanny. This was all too much. He panicked, and his mind got cloudy. Instead of seeing her chatter as excitement, it became overload, and his teeth started to chatter. So he put the brakes on. Now all of a sudden he was the one who wasn't ready.

He shared his feelings with his wife. Together they decided not to talk about Bugaboos, nannies, or bigger houses for at least a month. Of course, they still talked about upcoming little pitter-patter—but it was one step at a time. All the hubby needed was the space to step back to get in touch with his feelings on this new chapter of his life. And a month later, after being baby-talk-free, he came home excited to start a family.

What is this dance all about? Women like to talk about things that are on the way—like a pending engagement. The problem with all the chitchat is that it can overwhelm a guy. This dad-to-be felt so filled up with words he couldn't make sense of his own feelings. All the words were backing him into a corner. There was nowhere to turn, so he shut down. But once he had a little space (once she stopped talking about it), he was able to take a step back and see things clearly again. Sometimes a little space is all it takes.

When it comes to proposing—no matter who's doing the asking—both people have to be ready. If popping the question is not for you, there are ways you can encourage him along the way (read: encourage, not pressure). This will help you remain focused on (but not become obsessed with) reaching your goal for the relationship, while improving it. That way both parties will feel good about signing up for the long haul. There's a way to get through the limbo. It's when you as the couple have a healthy dynamic that you're on the right path to the altar.

GETTING THROUGH LIMBO

When I was in the middle of my own limbo, I discovered what was helping me get through it by noticing what was getting in the way. After being in a status-quo state for some time, I knew something in our relationship wasn't working. So I wanted to get to the bottom of it. The roadblocks that I discovered are all pretty common ones—different time frames, constant wedding talk, and expectations that we place on our beaus and ourselves. To combat these obstacles, I started to do the opposite of some of the behaviors that were getting me nowhere. I figured, it couldn't hurt.

- Instead of bringing it up several times a day, I zipped it (for as long as I possibly could).
- Instead of comparing the pace of my relationship to the pace of those whose weddings I was going to, I took time to think about how the pace of my relationship was working for me.
- Instead of focusing on what my beau could possibly be feeling, I took some time to get in touch with my own feelings.

To get to "I do," you both have to have the same goal in mind. You can be on the same page, but still moving at a different pace to get to the next chapter. And although men love a good race—racing to be ready for marriage is one they don't like. Here are a few things to keep in mind about what helps to get through the limbo.

LISTEN, DON'T REACT

Throughout your lives together as wife and husband, there will be plenty of difficult topics to talk about—the in-laws, kids with bad report cards, a bank account that isn't as hefty as you would like. And at times someone will get defensive and these conversations will go nowhere.

Start practicing how to get these conversations to go somewhere. When he shares his reasons for why he's not ready yet, we hear him being critical of us. ("If only I was good enough, then he would have proposed already!") When it comes down to it, a guy's reason for not proposing yet usually has nothing to do with his girlfriend personally.

If we really want to know what's on his mind and where he stands, it's important to manage our reactions. A response like

"Well, fine, then!" (with a door slam) will cue him that a conversation about getting engaged only leads to an argument. He doesn't want that, so he'll choose not to talk about it.

When he does talk, really listening to what he has to say will give you valuable information and insight into your relationship.

REMEMBER WHERE YOU COME FROM

Remember that you come from two different places. And I don't mean Boston and Dallas. I mean two different schools of thought. You say he has cold feet, while he says you have hot feet. It's not worth trying to convince one another who's ready too early and who's too late. You are where you are timewise because to you that's a reasonable place to be.

Let's take a stroll down memory lane: Where were you when you were seven years old? Playing dress-up, princess, and make-believe bride? How about at twelve? Was your notebook covered with doodles of your first name combined with the last name of the cute boy who sat in the fourth row in history class? How else would you know what it would look like when you got married? Jump ahead to age twenty-two. You were probably flipping through bridal magazines long before there was even a glimpse of a groom in the picture.

As for him, where was he when he was seven? Girls were icky back then—he was probably running around playing tag with his guy friends. And at twelve? Sitting behind a girl in math class and pulling her bra strap through her shirt. Flash ahead to age twenty-two. Probably going out to meet women (lots and lots of them).

So remember that when it comes to this marriage stuff, you very well may be in two different places. That's because you come from two different places. If your selected calendar dates about getting engaged are far apart, then negotiate. Meet halfway. If you both really want the engagement to happen, agree to each work toward a new time frame. One that's in the middle.

TAKE CONTROL

Why should he be the driver of the relationship? You're in this together. Instead of waiting for him to make up his mind about what it is that he wants, decide what it is that you want. Tired of waiting? Then set a time frame for yourself as to how much longer you will wait. This way you'll feel like you're taking control of the situation.

Women who feel they've stayed in a relationship a year or two too many end up feeling resentful and helpless. Stop focusing on what's taking him so long, and start focusing on what it is you'd like to do. Then you'll feel like you're navigating as well. Taking the passenger seat to let someone else lead the way feels powerless. You don't have to take the backseat. Be a copilot.

BREAK THE HABIT OF DROPPING HINTS

Asking your beau about engagement several times a day is a common habit. And right up there with biting your nails or tapping your pen, it's a tough one to break. It's a vicious cycle. The more you bring it up, the more time he adds to the proposal. The more he drags it out, the more you bring it up. Seems like the ring isn't the only circle here.

Dropping hints and having an actual talk about the next phase of your relationship are two completely different approaches. Whenever you drop hints, you're hoping he'll pick up on your subliminal messages. Guys don't always read between the lines to pick up on what it is you're trying to express. After all, when you hint around at what you want for your birthday, nine times out of ten he'll get you something else.

When I asked men what's the best way for a woman to bring up marriage chat, most men advised, "Directly."

The more women repeat themselves, the more men hear it as nagging. A sure way to make him zone out. Break the cycle by trading in the hints for setting a time to talk together.

DON'T COMPARE YOURSELF TO OTHERS

When we compare our relationship status to others, it gets in the way of our own security and happiness. When you say, "Everyone else is getting engaged," all he hears is you want a wedding because everyone else is planning one. Of course that's not your intention. But he starts to think your motivation is from the pressure you feel to be *someone's* wife, not necessarily *his* wife.

Women tend to gravitate toward wanting to do what they see their friends doing. Why else would we all pass around the latest issue of *Vogue*—to see what others are wearing. Or talk about our neighbor's most recent home improvements—to keep up with the Joneses. Or go with each other makeup shopping—to see the latest must-have shades.

This goes for getting engaged. We can't help but want to plan a wedding when all of our friends are scheduling cake tastings and going to bridal expos for the hottest gown fashions. What is it about being in sync? If we're not, somehow we feel left out.

Here's an example: I just got off the phone with a friend. We were having one of those "You wouldn't believe how much houses go for out here" conversations. She talked about what she spent for her house, compared to what our friends are paying. She said, "It makes me think I could have stretched a little more." I quickly jumped in with a pep talk about how she doesn't have to clean out the piggy bank for it to be a good investment just because that's what everyone else is choosing.

The same with getting engaged: It's important to get in touch with what it is that you want. Make a decision based on your own needs.

DON'T LET WANTING TO GET MARRIED TAKE OVER YOUR RELATIONSHIP

It's good to be focused. But when a focus turns into an obsession, it's sure to put a damper on your relationship and become a barricade to wedded bliss. I know that feeling ready to become engaged before your boyfriend is a big issue. Scratch that. It's a huge one. But letting the frustration you feel from being on two different time schedules seep into your entire relationship will take away from enjoying the good stuff. The candlelight dinners. ("Is the ring hidden in the dessert?") The long walks. ("Is it in his pocket?") The Sunday morning paper. ("Is it waiting for me wrapped in the funny pages?")

He'll start to see that no matter what he does, he's not able to make you happy. And it's probably true. The key to getting through this stage is to take control of the pre-engagement limbo rather than have it take over your relationship. So stay grounded.

FOOD FOR THOUGHT

The ingredients that get the relationship through pre-engagement limbo should be the same ingredients you'd find for a happy marriage.

My older cousin Michelle always has great tips—whether it's on decorating a home (she sets the table and it looks like a masterpiece), how to have a wonderful relationship with your kids, or how to enjoy a happy marriage. Naturally I wanted to hear what she had to say about ingredients for a successful life together as man and wife.

COUSIN MICHELLE'S TOP TEN INGREDIENTS FOR A HAPPY MARRIAGE

(With a Little Commentary by Yours Truly)

1. Remember that "We" comes before "I" in wedding. (Sounds like this one fits from pre- to post-wedding.)
2. Never go to bed angry. (A preventative measure against waking up on the wrong side of the bed.)
3. Talk to each other, not at each other, and never yell. (How can anyone hear through the yelling, anyway?)
4. Be a good listener and know when to keep your mouth shut. (We should pick our battles.)
5. Make reservations, and often. (Hopefully someplace romantic.)
6. Go away together at least two weekends a year. (Keep the spark alive.)
7. Have fulfilling activities as individuals. (A.k.a.: Make him miss you a little when you're out with the girls.)
8. Make date night a priority. (Continue to date each other—long after you're married.)
9. Invest in the marriage—you can't be good parents if you aren't a strong couple. (Your kids will thank you later.)
10. Have fun, hug and kiss, and tell the other person "I love you" as often as possible! (Who wouldn't love that!)

WHAT YOU SAID

Here's what others had to say about the most important ingredients for a happy marriage.

Communication (a majority response)
Trust
Friendship
Laughter
Honesty
Growing together
Sharing the same values
Feeling like you're part of a team
Balance

Trust, companionship, compatibility, having a best friend.
—MARCY, 28

• • •

Communication, spontaneity, romance, compromise, fun,
laughter, sense of humor, balance, division of labor
(but not tit for tat—that's different), being attracted to
one another. —EMILY, 31

• • •

Even though it might sound trite, communication is one of
the biggest. Also, learn how to give in. You don't always have
to be right. Some of the tiniest things create the biggest
power struggles. Don't forget just to be nice. Sometimes, just
asking, "Is something wrong?" can get you communicating
about something important. And last, don't always
defend yourself, just listen and respond. He's probably at
least partly right. —MARGIE, 40

Jill Bourque, creator of the hit improv comedy stage show *How
We First Met,* has been interviewing couples about their relationships for the past five years. I asked her what she sees as the most
important ingredients. She gave me this insight: "Over the past

five years I've had the opportunity to interview hundreds of couples live on stage about their relationships. And I've noticed some traits that happy couples share. I think one of the most important things is the willingness to grow as a couple—trying new things together and keeping a sense of humor. Laughter really is one of the best aphrodisiacs!"

You have the recipe. Now it's time to get cooking—but without turning up the heat on your man. It's important to remember there's someone in the kitchen with you, another chef who wants the dish to turn out delicious. So you have to work together.

Think of another time in your relationship when you couldn't agree on the same thing at the same time. When talking about a vacation, was he ever thinking surfing at the ocean and you wanted a mountain retreat? Or how about when you wanted to see the new hit comedy when he was leaning toward something with a little action? These were times when you had to compromise and meet somewhere in the middle so you'd both be happy. How did you do it? How did it turn out? If it turned out fine, what made it do so? If you couldn't agree, what was it that got in the way?

My Aunt Bev taught me that sometimes when you want two different things, you have to decide who it's more important to. And when it's important to both of you—compromise. Maybe you pick a vacation place that has something you both want. Or maybe you see the comedy now, and next time he gets to pick the flick. So when you both want to get engaged, but you'd like it a little sooner and he a little later, how about meeting in the middle and picking a time frame that feels good to both of you?

MY LITTLE LESSON ON COMPROMISE

My husband and I were in Bermuda for our honeymoon. We still had a few days left in our trip when the island got word that there was a hurricane warning in effect. The winds were picking up—and the storm would be arriving in two days. Guests started checking out. The hotel even suggested that if we could get on a flight, they would recommend us all departing. They didn't know how long the airport would be closed following the storm and assumed airline schedules would be a mess for the coming days. Of course my husband wanted to stay, and I wanted to go. We went back and forth and back and forth again on what to do. I made my argument. He made his. I'd make mine again. He'd rebut it. We left on the very last plane that would be taking off to Boston. We'd have a night in Boston before heading back to California. We arrived at Logan Airport and made our way to the baggage claim pickup. There was a TV crew doing a story on those who had cut their honeymoons short. The reporter asked my husband, "So why did you leave?" He said, "Actually I wanted to stay. But my wife wanted to leave. We decided to compromise. So we left."

He didn't realize that he had just given the reporter a great sound bite. The producer turned it into a story about how "this guy learned an early lesson on compromise right after getting married." They ran the piece, and it got picked up by other stations before landing on NPR.

WHEN WORLDS COLLIDE

When I was talking to the actor Kevin Burke, the star of *Defending the Caveman,* about this relationship stuff, he shared a line from the show: "Sometimes she has to step into his world. And he has to step into hers." And sometimes this needs to be done to help understand each other better about getting engaged. You may have grown up fantasizing about wedding-day dress-up, while he may have been fantasizing about the *Charlie's Angels* poster on his bedroom wall coming to life.

Could it be that we're programmed to want to domesticate, while he's programmed to run around unhitched? This doesn't mean that he doesn't want to be with you or that he doesn't love you. It just means that being with the same person for the rest of his life doesn't feel as natural for him—and it's a little scary. Just as much as you'd like him to understand that you bringing up engagement does not equal nagging, he'd like you to understand why he's not rushing to the altar.

> Communicating helps to get through the pre-engagement limbo. Really talk about what his issues are with the commitment, and talk about your issues with the commitment part too. Understand and respect each other's feelings. Try to understand what his fears are and where they come from. —STEPHANIE, 28

Notes from the Professor, Dr. Judye Hess

They say the best ingredient of a happy marriage is for two people to be best friends. If they have the kind of relationship in which they can talk about everything, then why does talking about getting engaged have to be so taboo?

YOUR PRE-ENGAGEMENT CHECKLIST

There are two main ingredients of getting through pre-engagement limbo.

One is to understand each other's differences. Know that sometimes a conflict can be brewing simply because you're coming from two different places. And second: Don't lose yourself in all of this. Think about what advice you'd give your best friend. In this case, make that best friend you.

1. **Have good communication.** If you can't communicate about getting engaged, how are you going to handle big conversations that will come up through life together as a married couple? Communication is key. It's one of the most important ingredients to make a happy marriage.

2. **Express what you want.** Don't nag about what you want, but share your feelings about what it is that you would like.

3. **Have patience.** Avoid bringing up the E-word every day. People in general can only take in so many words about the same topic. Your guy may like watching reruns on TV, but he definitely doesn't like dealing with reruns at home.

4. **Don't give him an ultimatum; give yourself one.** Setting a time frame for yourself will let you feel more in control.

5. **Know when it's time to keep him and when it's time to sweep him.** Keep your eyes and ears open. Don't forget we have the greatest gift of all—a woman's intuition.

6. **Keep a sense of humor.** This is a fun time in your life. Try to see each moment for what it is—a time when you're in love and possibly starting a future together.

7. **Know that you're not alone.** No matter how many weddings you're going to this summer, most of the brides probably felt ready to get engaged before the groom.

8. **Know how to get through an expectation downer with grace.** Don't let anticipation spoil the fun of what can otherwise be a fabulous moment.
9. **Don't hand over your power**—you can call your shots.
10. **Remember, the ingredients that make for a happy marriage also make for a happy pre-engagement phase.**

To answer the question "Are guys ever ready?"—well, we've all seen the look on a groom-to-be's face before he walks down the aisle. There's a reason why guests mutter, "He looks like he needs a drink." But then, at least with most of them, when the groom sees his bride for the first time, his face lights up and his fears appear to melt away. Then they begin the real story—marriage. A picture-perfect romance—that's where the real work begins.

References

Barbara Dafoe Whitehead and David Popenoe. "Why Men Won't Commit: Exploring Young Men's Attitudes About Sex, Dating, and Marriage." *The State of Our Unions: The Social Health of Marriage in America, 2002.* New Brunswick, NJ: The National Marriage Project at Rutgers University, 2002.

Dan Kiley. *The Peter Pan Syndrome: Men Who Have Never Grown Up."* New York: Dodd, Mead, 1983.

Robert Fulghum. *All I Really Need to Know I Learned in Kindergarten.* New York: Villard Books, 1988.

Malcolm Gladwell. *The Tipping Point: How Little Things Can Make a Big Difference.* New York: Back Bay Books, 2000.

John Gray. *Men Are from Mars, Women Are from Venus.* New York: HarperCollins, 2002.

For more information on T-Group sensitivity training, started by Kurt Lewin and a team of social psychologists after World War II, visit the National Training Laboratories Web site at www.ntl.org.

To learn more about Dr. Judye Hess's work, visit
www.psychotherapist.com/judyehess/.

To learn more about Dr. Beth Miller's work on resilience, visit
www.bouncingback.org.

For more on Al Capp and the *Li'l Abner* comic strip, visit
www.lil-abner.com.

For more about Kevin Burke of *Defending the Caveman,* visit
www.cavemania.com.

For more about Jill Bourque's improv show, visit
www.howwefirstmet.com.

For "Economics A–Z," visit www.economist.com.

For *The Old Farmer's Almanac,* visit www.almanac.com.